Dedicated to

thousands of youths and adults who
are making a difference in the world by
demonstrating
the power of love,

and to all those
who have given me wise counsel
and strong encouragement
to examine my life and words
and to search out and apply
the rich teachings of Scripture
so that I can experience more
of the exceeding greatness
of God's power.

©2000 Institute in Basic Life Principles
Box One • Oak Brook, Illinois 60522-3001
Cover Design: Josh Williams
Artist: Stan Stein
Artwork reprinted by permission of The Friends of Israel Gospel Ministry, Inc.

ISBN 0-916888-18-5

270.1
G684s
c.1

2

the Sevenfold POWER
of First-Century
Churches *and* Homes

The Law Was Used to Bring Conviction
The Appeal Was Made to the Conscience
They "Called Out" for Salvation
The Need for Baptism Was Taught

How Does Unworthiness Produce Disease?
How to Have Effective Communion Services
An Example of a Character Examination
The Deeper Significance of Communion
The Power of Communion in Small Churches
The Requirement of a Clear Conscience
How Often Should Communion Be Observed?

What Name Describes God's Church?
How Prayer Unites the Body of Christ
How Prayer Can Serve Entire Communities
What Are the Types of Prayer?
Ten Dangers That Cause Leaders to Fall
The Importance of Positions in Prayer
The Power of Praying "in Jesus' Name"
The Key to Praying With Power

How Good Works Follow Fervent Prayer
How Believers Were Designed for Good Works
What Constitutes a Good Work?
How to "Do Good Unto All"
The Principle of Serving Under Authority
Is the Church to Serve or to Be Served?

A WINDOW OF OPPORTUNITY

As marriages and families in America continue to collapse, state agencies are overwhelmed with a huge caseload dealing with abused children, delinquent youths, domestic violence, unwed mothers, teenage gangs, drug abuse, and now, school and church massacres.

The lack of results in most court-appointed programs and the high recidivism in juvenile detention centers and adult prisons have forced agency officials to look for new and better answers. The new buzzwords are "privatization" and "faith-based groups."

The director of a child abuse center in one state made a startling confession: "Fifteen years ago, when I began working in this agency, I thought the government had all the answers and the Church had none. Now I realize that we have no answers and that we are open to any group that does."[1]

Ironically, government officials are looking to the Church for answers at a time when the general public is ridiculing Christianity. Yes, there is swift and firm reaction to anyone who would mock or joke about any minority group—except for Christians.

There is Biblical support for this public ridicule. Jesus stated that we are the salt of the earth and the light of the world, but "if the salt have lost his savour, wherewith shall it be salted?

it is thenceforth good for nothing, but to be cast out, and to be trodden under foot of men."[2]

There is little doubt or debate about the fact that the Church has lost its ability to retard evil. A shocking report by the Barna Research Group reveals that based on 131 indicators of conduct and philosophy, there is little difference between those who attend church and those who do not.[3]

The Church has lost its power because it has strayed far from the original plan and program that Jesus Christ established in the first Church. However, that plan has the same potential in the twenty-first century as it did in the first century.

The purpose of this book is to identify the factors that made the early Church so dynamic and to suggest practical ways that those factors can be restored in churches and homes today. By doing so, we can effectively meet the challenges and opportunities that are being given to us by leaders throughout the world.

We will discover that the world is not ridiculing the true message of Jesus Christ but rather the false and distorted expressions of it by those who claim to be His followers.

There was great hostility toward Jesus Christ in Jerusalem, to the point that the multitude clamored for His death and chose the release of a criminal.

Yet, when they experienced the love and truth of His followers, that same multitude repented and believed on the Lord Jesus Christ and impacted the world with God's way of life.

When ...

does a gathering
of believers
become a local church?

This book is not intended to be an exhaustive discourse on the local church. Nor is it designed to deal with the many facets of church government, policies, or practices.

It is intended to identify the key factors that made the first-century Church so dynamic and to suggest how these factors could be applied to churches in our day.

What actually constitutes a local church? Does a local church occur every time a group of believers meets together?

Such a gathering would have the presence of the Lord Jesus Christ, because He promised, "Where two or three are gathered together in my name, there am I in the midst of them."[4] However, is such a gathering a local church?

Consider which of the following factors would be necessary before a gathering of believers could be considered an authentic local church. Also, identify which factors were not present in the first church.

* *Does a name establish a church?*

* *Does a building constitute a church?*

* *Does a constitution make a church?*

* *Do members make a church?*

* *Do church elders make a church?*

* *Does baptizing authenticate a church?*

* *Does communion constitute a church?*

* *Does having a pastor make a church?*

* *Does ordination validate a church?*

* *Does church discipline make a church?*

* *Do offerings establish a church?*

* *Does sending missionaries make a church?*

A true local church is . . .

defined and demonstrated in the Book of Acts. The first church was established without a name, a building, or a constitution, but its members had the power of the Holy Spirit in their leaders, their converts, their message, their fellowship, their communion, their prayers, and their outreach. This sevenfold power of local churches and homes provides a clear pattern for genuine local churches in any century.

The Concept of "The House of God"

God refers to His Church as a house: "That thou mayest know how thou oughtest to behave thyself in the house of God, which is the church of the living God, the pillar and ground of the truth."[5]

God built the house of the Church, the "house" of each family unit, and the "house" of state. Each house has a divinely ordained structure of authority; and each house has a sphere of jurisdiction.

It is important to identify God's design for each house and to build it according to that design. For "except the Lord build the house, they labour in vain that build it."[6]

When . . .
does a local church cease
to be a true local church?

The Book of Revelation begins with seven messages to seven local churches in Asia. Each church is symbolized by a golden candlestick. This fact is made very clear in verse 20 of chapter 1: "The seven candlesticks which thou sawest are the seven churches."

Each church was praised for what it was doing right and most were reproved for specific areas in which they were lacking. However, the message to the church of Ephesus is particularly significant. They were told to repent of failure in a specific area. If they did not repent, God warned that He would come quickly and remove their candlestick out of its place.

The failure of this church was that they had left their first love. Genuine love is the power of the Spirit, and it is what made the first Church such a dynamic force in the world. Any local church that loses its power of love, loses its standing as a true local church. As was the case with the church of Ephesus, "He that hath an ear, let him hear what the Spirit saith unto the churches."[7]

A local church is . . .

a group of believers bonded together by a new birth in the Lord Jesus Christ for the purpose of edifying each other according to the Word of God and endued with the power of the Holy Spirit so that they can effectively carry out the work of God in the world. (See Ephesians 3:10, Colossians 1:12–29.)

God has given leaders to the Church "for the perfecting of the saints, for the work of the ministry, for the edifying of the body of Christ: Till we all come in the unity of the faith, and of the knowledge of the Son of God, unto a perfect man, unto the measure of the stature of the fulness of Christ . . . From whom the whole body fitly joined together and compacted by that which every joint supplieth, according to the effectual working in the measure of every part, maketh increase of the body unto the edifying of itself in love."[8]

The authenticity of a local church is determined by the power of the Holy Spirit as expressed in truth and love.[9] The first-century churches demonstrated this power, and the Apostle Paul's epistle to the church of Ephesus gave special emphasis to the importance of building their church around the power of God's love.

"That Christ may dwell in your hearts by faith; that ye, being rooted and grounded in love, May be able to comprehend with all saints what is the breadth, and length, and depth, and height; And to know the love of Christ."[10]

A church cannot be expected to rise above the spiritual level of its leaders.

"Let the elders that rule well be counted worthy of double honour, especially they who labour in the word and doctrine."

—I Timothy 5:17

THE POWER OF ITS LEADERS

Chapter Summary

A leader may have the fullness of God's Spirit in him, but he is not ready for ministry until the Holy Spirit is upon him in "power."[11] The apostles received the fullness of the Spirit after the resurrection of Christ. They were then given a test of obedience, followed by the power of the Spirit on the Day of Pentecost. This same pattern is seen in the life of Christ. He was "filled" with the Spirit at His baptism and then led by the Spirit into testing. He returned in the "power" of the Spirit, and the fame of His ministry spread throughout the entire region. The power of the Holy Spirit is the greatest force on earth—it is love!

WHY GOD CHOOSES UNLIKELY LEADERS

God often chooses the most unlikely candidates to be His leaders. God's purpose is to demonstrate to the leaders and others that their power comes from Him and not from themselves.

When the elders and rulers of the people of Israel realized the power of the good work done in making the lame man whole, and "when they saw the boldness of Peter and John, and perceived that they were unlearned and ignorant men, they marvelled; and they took knowledge of them, that they had been with Jesus."[12]

The Apostle Paul affirms this fact: "For ye see your calling, brethren, how that not many wise men after the flesh, not many mighty, not many noble, are called: But God hath chosen the foolish things of the world to confound the wise; and God hath chosen the weak things of the world to confound the things which are mighty; And base things of the world, and things which are despised, hath God chosen, yea, and things which are not, to bring to nought things that are: That no flesh should glory in his presence."[13]

Paul himself was, by his own testimony, the most unlikely of all believers to be a leader in the Church. He confessed that he was the chief of sinners,[14] and "he made havoc of the church, entering into every house, and haling men and women committed them to prison."[15]

THE LEAST, THE LITTLEST, AND THE LAST

God has a way of choosing the least, the littlest, and the last. When God called Gideon to lead the nation of Israel out of bondage, he exclaimed, "I am the least in my father's house."[16] When Saul was chosen to be king, he was amazed and asked, "Am not I a Benjamite, of the smallest of the tribes of Israel? and my family the least of all the families of the tribe of Benjamin?"[17] When Paul was ordained to be an apostle, he declared, "For I am the least of the apostles, that am not meet to be called an apostle, because I persecuted the church of God."[18] Those who recognize that they are least in the kingdom of God are candidates for God's power, which will make them the greatest in His kingdom. God chose Israel when they were a little people group in the land. "The LORD did not set his love upon you, nor choose you, because ye were more in number than any people; for ye were the fewest of all people."[19] Bethlehem was chosen as the birthplace of Christ and identified as "little among the thousands of Judah."[20]

When Saul was chosen by God to be king, Saul was "little" in his own eyes: "When thou wast little in thine own sight, wast thou not made the head of the tribes of Israel, and the LORD anointed thee king over Israel?"[21] When Solomon began his reign as king he stated, "I am but a little child: I know not how to go out or come in."[22] Jesus said a requirement to be great in the kingdom of Heaven was to humble one's self and become as a little child.[23]

David was the last child born to Jesse. Paul was the last apostle. The apostles were set apart to be last, and Jesus said that in the kingdom of God "many that are first shall be last; and the last shall be first."[24]

THE SECRET OF A LEADER'S POWER

The power of a spiritual leader is the *dunamis* of the Holy Spirit upon his life. Jesus carefully trained and prepared His disciples to experience this power, and through it to build His Church and impact the world. There are three important phases of experiencing this power.

The first phase is to be indwelt and filled by the Holy Spirit. The indwelling of the Spirit takes place at salvation, when "the Spirit itself beareth witness with our spirit that we are the children of God."[25]

As believers, we are to "be filled with the Spirit."[26] This command is in the present tense, which indicates continuous action. Since God's Spirit already indwells our spirit, this command would relate to our soul (*pseuche*), which involves our mind, will, and emotions. We receive the filling of the Holy Spirit by simply asking our Heavenly Father for it. "If ye then, being evil, know how to give good gifts unto your children: how much more shall your heavenly Father give the Holy Spirit to them that ask him?"[27]

Once we are indwelt and filled with the Holy Spirit, we are to yield the members of our body to Him for His control. "As ye have yielded your members servants to uncleanness and to iniquity unto iniquity; even so now yield your members servants to righteousness unto holiness."[28]

The Holy Spirit will then direct us into a time of testing. The test involves thanking God for the test,[29] rejoicing in it,[30] and obeying the Word of God as directed by the Holy Spirit.[31]

If we pass this test, we will receive the power (*dunamis*) of the Holy Spirit. In preparation for this testing, God will give us sufficient grace to overcome. Grace is the desire and power that God gives to do His will. Paul attaches power to grace in passages such as the following: "But by the grace of God I am what I am: and his grace which was bestowed upon me was not in vain; but I laboured more abundantly than they all: yet not I, but the grace of God which was with me."[32] He will also give us counsel and encouragement through the Scriptures, so we can respond to temptations as Jesus did by quoting the Scriptures, which are the sword of the Spirit.[33]

To the degree that we pass the test, by thanking God for it and rejoicing in it, we experience the power of the Holy Spirit upon us. We are then able to demonstrate the fruit of the Holy Spirit, which begins with love, joy, and peace.[34]

Notice how each of these elements is mentioned by Paul in his praise of the Macedonian believers. He first noted "the grace of God bestowed" on them. Then he explained how they went through "a great trial of affliction." The immediate result was that their joy and their love abounded through their generosity to other believers. He related this directly to the power of the Holy Spirit upon them. "To their power *(dunamis)* I bear record."[35]

After Jesus Christ rose from the dead and before He ascended into Heaven, He appeared to His disciples and "breathed on them, and saith unto them, Receive ye the Holy Ghost."[36] There is no doubt that they then had the Holy Spirit in them.

However, having the Spirit "in" them was not sufficient for leadership in Christ's Church. Therefore, Jesus instructed them to wait in Jerusalem until they were "endued with power" by the Holy Spirit.[37]

The Greek word for "endued" is *enduo*, which means "clothe (with)."[38] The word for "power" is the Greek word *dunamis*.[39] The English equivalents to *dunamis* are the words *dynamo, dynamite,* and *dynamic.*

THE TESTS THAT TURN "FILLING" INTO POWER

What made the difference between the filling of the Holy Spirit, which Jesus gave to His disciples when He breathed upon them, and the power of the Holy Spirit, which came upon them in the upper room? It was their faithfulness in a test of obedience.

After they received the Holy Spirit, the disciples were given a command: "Tarry ye in the city of

Jerusalem."[40] Waiting upon the Lord in prayer, fasting, and the study of the Word can be difficult when many other tasks may seem more interesting or desirable. The disciples had already failed to wait even one hour in the garden. The result was their shameful abandonment and denial of the Lord at His greatest time of need. However, they now passed the test of obedience and received the power of the Spirit that was foretold by the prophet Joel.[41]

Jesus illustrates this threefold sequence in His own life and ministry. He was filled with the Holy Spirit at His baptism.[42] He was then led by the Spirit into the wilderness to face His test of obedience. After successfully passing this test by quoting Scripture to Satan, He returned in the "power" of the Spirit.

Here is the account: "And Jesus being full of the Holy Ghost returned from Jordan, and was led by the Spirit into the wilderness."[43] After his testing, He "returned in the power of the Spirit into Galilee: and there went out a fame of him through all the region round about."[44] Notice that it was after He returned in the power of the Spirit that His ministry and fame spread throughout the region.

The pattern of testing after filling was also demonstrated among the Thessalonian believers. They received the Holy Spirit at salvation. "For our gospel came not unto you in word only, but also in power *(dunamis)* and in the Holy Ghost and in much assurance."[45]

They then went through testing. They "received the word in much affliction."[46] The result of passing the test with joy is described in II Thessalonians 1:3–4, "Your faith groweth exceedingly, and the charity of every one of you all toward each other aboundeth; So that we ourselves glory in you in the churches of God for your patience and faith in all your persecutions and tribulations that ye endure."

We see an interesting parallel of this threefold sequence in Creation. When man was created, it was a corporate act of the Trinity. "Let us make man in our image."[47] However, Jesus is honored as the chief Creator: "All things were made by him; and without him was not anything made that was made."[48] Therefore, Jesus "formed man of the dust of the ground, and breathed into his nostrils the breath of life; and man became a living soul."[49]

After Adam received the breath of life, he was given a test of obedience. "And the LORD God commanded the man, saying, Of every tree of the garden thou mayest freely eat: But of the tree of the knowledge of good and evil, thou shalt not eat of it."[50] Adam failed the test and lost the potential that he could have had when he would have eaten from the tree of life.

Another pattern of this sequence is pictured by the nation of Israel's coming out of the bondage of Egypt. Egypt is a type of the world and the passing through the Red Sea is symbolic of baptism.[51]

After their "baptism," the nation was given tests of obedience in the wilderness. They failed these tests and perished without reaching their promised land.

Their children were given a second chance. They passed through the "baptism" of the River Jordan and were given a series of tests to conquer the land of Canaan. To the degree that they were obedient, they had power to conquer. When they disobeyed, they lost that power.

After receiving the Holy Spirit and being baptized, every believer should expect to go through tests of tribulation. "Yea, and all that will live godly in Christ Jesus shall suffer persecution."[52]

If we pass the test by thanking God for the trials and rejoicing in them, we will experience the *dunamis* of the Holy Spirit. "In every thing give thanks: for this is the will of God in Christ Jesus concerning you."[53] "Rejoice in the Lord alway: and again I say, Rejoice."[54]

A NEW UNDERSTANDING OF TRIALS

Tests of obedience are required before believers experience the power of the Holy Spirit. This insight gives new meaning to the joy and excitement that the first-century Christians had when they went through their tribulations.[55]

No wonder Jesus told His disciples, "Blessed are ye, when men shall revile you, and persecute you, and shall say all manner of evil against you falsely, for my sake. Rejoice, and be exceeding glad: for great is your reward in heaven: for so persecuted they the prophets which were before you."[56]

The comparison that Jesus made between persecuted Christians and Old Testament prophets is significant as it relates to the Holy Spirit. Isaiah testified, "The spirit of the Lord GOD is upon me; because the LORD hath anointed me to preach good tidings unto the meek; he hath sent me to bind up the brokenhearted, to proclaim liberty to the captives, and the opening of the prison to them that are bound."[57] Jesus quoted these very verses in the synagogue of Nazareth shortly after He returned from the wilderness in the power of the Spirit.[58]

The power of God's Spirit is further explained in Isaiah 11:2: "And the spirit of the LORD shall rest upon him, the spirit of wisdom and understanding, the spirit of counsel and might, the spirit of knowledge and of the fear of the LORD."

The Apostle Paul discovered this power of God's Spirit when he asked God to remove an infirmity from him. Paul understood that it was through this very infirmity that he would experience the power of the Holy Spirit, provided that he rejoiced in the infirmity. Paul responded, "Most gladly therefore will I rather glory in my infirmities, that the power of Christ may rest upon me."[59]

Paul then identified five types of trials that will produce the power of Christ if we thank God for them and rejoice in what God can do through them. "Therefore I take pleasure in infirmities, in reproaches, in necessities, in persecutions, in distresses for Christ's sake: for when I am weak, then am I strong."[60]

James begins his epistle with this important truth: "My brethren, count it all joy when ye fall into divers temptations; Knowing this, that the trying of your faith worketh patience. But let patience have her perfect work, that ye may be perfect and entire, wanting nothing."[61]

Peter also emphasized the importance of trials of obedience before receiving the glory of God's power. "When ye do well, and suffer for it, ye take it patiently, this is acceptable with God. For even hereunto were ye called: because Christ also suffered for us, leaving us an example, that ye should follow his steps."[62]

Peter keeps reaffirming this important truth, "Beloved, think it not strange concerning the fiery trial which is to try you, as though some strange thing happened unto you: But rejoice, inasmuch as ye are partakers of Christ's sufferings; that, when his glory shall be revealed, ye may be glad also with exceeding joy. If ye be reproached for the name of Christ, happy are ye; for the spirit of glory and of God resteth upon you: on their part he is evil spoken of, but on your part he is glorified."[63]

The first-century Christians took the spoiling of their goods with joy.[64] They knew that if they rejoiced in the distress of having their property damaged, they would experience a greater measure of the power of the Holy Spirit and with that power they would be able to accomplish significant things for God and others. The eternal rewards of these achievements would be far more valuable than any earthly possessions they might have lost.

With this in mind, Paul declared, "I reckon that the sufferings of this present time are not worthy to be compared with the glory which shall be revealed in us."[65]

THE SPIRIT OF GLORY AND OF GOD

What an amazing promise! If we are reproached for the name of Christ, "the spirit of glory and of God resteth upon us."[66] In the lives of those who reproach, God's ways are ridiculed, but if we rejoice because of it, God gives us a spirit of glory.

This is no small reward. It is what Paul speaks of when he says, "But we all, with open face beholding as in a glass the glory of the Lord, are changed into the same image from glory to glory, even as by the Spirit of the Lord."[67] And again, "For God, who commanded the light to shine out of darkness, hath shined in our hearts, to give the light of the knowledge of the glory of God in the face of Jesus Christ."[68]

The Greek word for *glory* is *doxa*,[69] from which we get the word *doxology*. It means to render esteem, praise, honor, and worship. Jesus glorified the Father through His obedience to crucifixion and the resulting radiance of His resurrection.

Our ultimate glory will be experienced in Heaven, but a foretaste of that glory will "rest upon" us as we respond correctly to reproaches and tribulations in this life.[70]

WHAT IS THE POWER OF THE HOLY SPIRIT?

What is the "dunamis" of the Holy Spirit? It is the most powerful force on the face of the earth—it is genuine love.

We know that God is love. We also recognize Jesus as love, because He demonstrated the highest form of love by dying an excruciating death on the cross for our sin.[71] Yet we do not often think of the Holy Spirit in terms of love. We know that He inspired men to write the Scriptures, He guides us unto all truth,[72] and He convicts "the world of sin, and of righteousness, and of judgment."[73] Yet His primary attribute is love. It is mentioned first in the list of His fruit: "But the fruit of the Spirit is love, joy, peace . . . ."[74]

The angry mobs that demanded the death of Jesus were transformed into dynamic disciples because they experienced the love of God through the power of the Holy Spirit.

Leaders may have great eloquence, deep understanding, and sacrificial deeds. However, if they do not have the love of the Holy Spirit, they are as "sounding brass, or a tinkling cymbal."[75]

The relationship between the Holy Spirit, obedience, and love is taught in many passages. "Peter, an apostle of Jesus Christ, to the strangers scattered . . . Elect according to the foreknowledge of God the Father, through sanctification of the Spirit, unto obedience and sprinkling of the blood of Jesus Christ: Grace unto you, and peace, be multiplied."[76]

The grace of God is the powerful working of the Holy Spirit, especially in the life of a leader. Paul testified, "Whereof I was made a minister, according to the gift of the grace of God given unto me by the effectual working of his power."[77]

The dynamic of the Spirit, obedience, and the power of love is also presented in the following passage: "Seeing ye have purified your souls in obeying the truth through the Spirit unto unfeigned love of the brethren, see that ye love one another with a pure heart fervently."[78]

Church leaders who speak the truth without love can cause their hearers to react to the message and reject the very love of Christ. On the other hand, those who try to be loving but do not speak the truth are compromisers and contradict the very love they profess to preach.

Peter spoke firm words of truth to the thousands who at first mocked the disciples as being full of wine.[79] "Ye men of Israel, hear these words; Jesus of Nazareth, a man approved of God among you by miracles and wonders and signs . . . ye have taken, and by wicked hands have crucified and slain."[80] Yet at the same time he spoke with a powerful spirit of love and appeal. He spoke to them as "men and brethren"[81] and patiently reasoned with them using Old Testament Scriptures.

"For God hath not given us the spirit of fear; but of power, and of love, and of a sound mind."[82] In this passage the spirit of power and love are linked together around a "sound mind," which is defined in Greek as "discipline and self-control"[83] —two basic aspects of obedience.

THE POWER TO DO "GREATER THINGS"

Jesus assured His disciples that after He returned to Heaven, they would be able to do greater things than He did because He would send them the Holy Spirit.

"Verily, verily, I say unto you, He that believeth on me, the works that I do shall he do also; and greater works than these shall he do; because I go unto my Father. . . . And I will pray the Father, and he shall give you another Comforter, that he may abide with you for ever."[84]

It sounds incredible that the disciples would do greater works than Jesus. Who could do a greater work than giving sight to the blind, causing the deaf to hear, cleansing lepers, and raising the dead?[85] Yet there is an important sense in which this is true. The greatest work in the world is for God's Spirit to transform cold, hard, unrepentant hearts into loving, forgiving worshipers of Christ.

The loving power of the Holy Spirit flowing through the yielded, obedient believer has the capability of turning men's hearts to the Lord and redeeming their souls for all eternity.

Raising people from the dead, feeding five thousand men, and healing diseases are all matters that primarily affect this life. However, the transformation of hearts and minds of people so they respond to the love of Jesus Christ brings salvation, which lasts for all eternity.

EXAMPLES OF LEADERS WITH THE POWER OF LOVE

Every experience of being endued with power is not necessarily the same. Each person is a unique creation of God, and God works through each individual in different ways to accomplish

His will. Yet every anointing of the Spirit will be accompanied by a demonstration of God's love. One such example is that of D. L. Moody. Notice how love was the result of God's Spirit upon him.

> One day, in the city of New York— oh, what a day!—I cannot describe it, I seldom refer to it; it is almost too sacred an experience to name. . . . I can only say that God revealed Himself to me, and I had such an experience of His love that I had to ask Him to stay His hand.
>
> I went to preaching again. The sermons were not different; I did not present new truths, and yet hundreds were converted. I would not now be placed back where I was before that blessed experience if you should give me all the world.[86]

Charles Finney had an amazing ministry in the nineteenth century. Hundreds of thousands came to Christ through his preaching, including instances in which entire communities were converted or impacted by the Gospel. He gives a detailed report of what happened when he received the anointing of the Holy Spirit.

> . . . The Holy Spirit descended upon me in a manner that seemed to go through me, body and soul. I could feel the impression, like a wave of electricity, going through and through me. Indeed, it seemed to come in waves and waves of liquid love . . . .
>
> No words can express the wonderful love that was shed abroad in my

heart. I wept aloud with joy and love . . . . These waves came over me, and over me, and over me, one after the other, until I recollect I cried out, "I shall die if these waves continue to pass over me!"[87]

When Charles Finney went to preach after this experience he stated, "The spirit of God came upon me with such power, that it was like opening a battery upon them. . . . The Holy spirit fell upon the congregation in a most remarkable manner."[88]

How the Holy Spirit Is Received

The Holy Spirit is a person of the Trinity. He enters a believer's life at salvation and bears witness with our spirits that each of us is a child of God.[89] Man also has a soul. "I pray God your whole spirit and soul and body be preserved blameless unto the coming of our Lord Jesus Christ."[90] The soul also must be filled with the Holy Spirit.

This can be accomplished by simply asking our Heavenly Father for the filling of His Spirit. "If ye then, being evil, know how to give good gifts unto your children: how much more shall your heavenly Father give the Holy Spirit to them that ask him?"[91]

In addition to the indwelling of the Holy Spirit in our spirit and the filling of the Holy Spirit in our soul,[92] we need to have the control of the Holy Spirit in our bodily members[93] so that we will walk in obedience to the Holy Spirit.[94]

Five Tests That Produce Power

In the same way that David chose from five smooth stones to conquer Goliath,[95] so the Holy

Spirit chooses from five types of tests to topple the giant of pride in our lives. From our state of recognized weakness, we are able to receive the power of the Holy Spirit upon us.

The Apostle Paul gives a marvelous description of how this procedure worked in his own life. Paul was filled with the Holy Spirit, and through the Spirit, he received marvelous revelations of truth. Yet there was still further power that both the Holy Spirit and Paul knew was needed for continued and increased effectiveness in ministry. The Holy Spirit chose the test of infirmity to test Paul's obedience.

Three times Paul prayed that this thorn in the flesh would be removed from him. However, God explained that it was not to be removed. This infirmity was actually given to Paul so that more power could come upon his life. Once Paul understood this, he eagerly embraced his infirmity, and in fact, he gloried in it and thanked God for what He would do through it.

"And lest I should be exalted above measure through the abundance of the revelations, there was given to me a thorn in the flesh, the messenger of Satan to buffet me, lest I should be exalted above measure. For this thing I besought the Lord thrice, that it might depart from me. And he said unto me, My grace is sufficient for thee: for my strength is made perfect in weakness.

"Most gladly therefore will I rather glory in my infirmities, that the power of Christ may rest upon me. Therefore I take pleasure in infirmities, in reproaches, in necessities, in persecutions, in distresses for Christ's sake: for when I am weak, then am I strong."[96] The five items in Paul's list are used by the Holy Spirit to bring about His power, and we would do well to take a closer look at each one.

1. Infirmities

The Greek word for *infirmities* is *astheneia*.[97] It means "feebleness (of body or mind)." By implication, it is a physical malady, disease, or sickness. This will take place in every person's life, because we dwell in mortal bodies that will experience increasing disability. Yet even in this, Paul pointed out, "For which cause we faint not; but though our outward man perish, yet the inward man is renewed day by day."[98]

2. Reproaches

The Greek word for *reproaches* is *hubris*.[99] It refers to insults, verbal injury, slander, gossip, verbal abuse, scorn, and ridicule. Reproach is painful, and our natural tendency is to react to it with equal venom. Yet Scripture warns about "not rendering evil for evil, or railing for railing: but contrariwise blessing; knowing that ye are thereunto called, that ye should inherit a blessing."[100] The blessing is the spirit of glory and the power of love.

3. Necessities

This word simply describes the needful burdens in life that must be carried out in fulfilling our personal and work responsibilities.

4. Persecutions

A persecutor is one who stalks his victim like a predator and creates trouble and reaction wherever possible. Paul's persecutors followed him from city to city.

5. Distresses

The Greek word for *distress* is *stenochoria*,[101]

which is metaphorically defined as dire calamity or extreme affliction. It would include calamities, anguish, grief, and great sorrow. If one member of a family has a disabling infirmity, the other family members will experience distress.

How to Pass the Test of Obedience

We have already noted that we pass the test of all these trials and tribulations if we obey the command of the Lord to thank God for them and rejoice in them while remaining faithful to the Word of God and the guidance of the Holy Spirit.

The instruction of Philippians 4:4 is not a suggestion for better living; it is a double command. "Rejoice in the Lord alway: and again I say, Rejoice."

The very will of God for a believer is to thank God in whatever experience He allows. "In every thing give thanks: for this is the will of God in Christ Jesus concerning you."[102]

When tribulations came upon first-century Christians, they rejoiced in the hope of experiencing the power of the Holy Spirit. With that power of love, the Holy Spirit would be able to accomplish mighty things in and through them that would result in eternal rewards.

This was the message that Paul gave them: We "rejoice in hope of the glory of God. And not only so, but we glory in tribulations also: knowing that tribulation worketh patience; And patience, experience; and experience, hope: And hope maketh not ashamed; because the love of God is shed abroad in our hearts by the Holy Ghost which is given unto us."[103]

Satan loves to take the trials that God allows for increased power and instead get us to murmur and complain about them. This is precisely what happened to the nation of Israel in the wilderness. God led them out of Egypt because they cried out to Him in their bondage. But then, whenever they faced a new test, they were not thankful for what God had already done, nor did they cry out to God for His continued provision. Instead, they complained about their plight and murmured against Moses and Aaron.

Moses made it clear that their murmurings were not against him, but against God. "And Moses said, This shall be, when the LORD shall give you in the evening flesh to eat, and in the morning bread to the full; for that the LORD heareth your murmurings which ye murmur against him: and what are we? your murmurings are not against us, but against the LORD."[104]

Paul warns that if a believer fails to rejoice in the trials that come, he will most likely respond in anger, wrath, or malice. This will in turn give authority to Satan to bring about physical and spiritual destruction. Therefore, he warns, "Let not the sun go down upon your wrath: Neither give place to the devil."[105]

How an Infirmity Produced Greater Love

After writing out the truths in this chapter, the Lord illustrated how the power of love can result from a physical trial. It occurred in a way I had never experienced before. At about 10:30 in the morning, I felt a sharp pain on my right side. It was more severe than anything I had ever felt. I assumed that it would pass in a few moments, but instead it got worse. Hour after hour, I experienced body-wrenching pain.

There was no relief. If I lay down, it got worse. If I sat or stood, it was just as bad. A doctor informed me that, based on the symptoms, it was a kidney stone. After twenty hours of excruciating agony, it finally passed. Suddenly, I had a new understanding and love for those who are unsaved.[106]

I remembered the account of Lazarus and the rich man: "In hell he lift up his eyes, being in torments, and seeth Abraham afar off, and Lazarus in his bosom. And he cried and said, Father Abraham, have mercy on me, and send Lazarus, that he may dip the tip of his finger in water, and cool my tongue; for I am tormented in this flame."[107]

I suddenly realized that the torment I had for just twenty hours was representative of the torment that would be experienced by those in hell for millions and millions of years—they would have no relief. It is significant that the rich man wanted a little relief for his tongue, which suggests that the member of the body that will suffer the most in hell is that which does the most damage on earth.[108] This experience also gave me new appreciation for the testimony of the Apostle Paul when he spoke of his thorn in the flesh. "My strength is made perfect in weakness. Most gladly therefore will I rather glory in my infirmities, that the power of Christ may rest upon me."[109]

Notes

1. Director of Shelter for Abused Children in Oklahoma City, OK.
2. Matthew 5:13.
3. The Barna Report for November/December 1997, *The American Witness*, The Barna Research Group.
4. Matthew 18:20.
5. I Timothy 3:15.
6. Psalm 127:1.
7. Revelation 2:17.
8. Ephesians 4:12–16.
9. See John 13:35.
10. Ephesians 3:17–19.
11. Luke 4:1–14.
12. Acts 4:13–14.
13. I Corinthians 1:26–29.
14. I Timothy 1:15.
15. Acts 8:3.
16. Judges 6:15.
17. I Samuel 9:21.
18. I Corinthians 15:9.
19. Deuteronomy 7:6–7.
20. See Micah 5:2.
21. I Samuel 15:17.
22. I Kings 3:7.
23. Matthew 18:4.
24. Matthew 19:30.
25. Romans 8:16.
26. Ephesians 5:18.
27. Luke 11:13.
28. Romans 6:19.
29. I Thessalonians 5:18.
30. Philippians 4:4.
31. Galatians 5:16.
32. I Corinthians 15:10.
33. Matthew 4.
34. Galatians 5:22.
35. II Corinthians 8:1–3.
36. John 20:22.
37. Luke 24:49.
38. James Strong, S.T.D., LL.D, *Strong's Exhaustive Concordance of the Bible*, McDonald Publishing Company, McClean, Virginia, #1746.
39. Ibid., #1411.
40. Luke 24:49.
41. Acts 2:1–21.
42. Mark 1:9–11.
43. Luke 4:1.
44. Luke 4:14.
45. I Thessalonians 1:5.
46. I Thessalonians 1:6.
47. Genesis 1:26.
48. John 1:3. (See Colossians 1:16.)
49. Genesis 2:7.
50. Genesis 2:16–17.
51. I Corinthians 10:1–6.
52. II Timothy 3:12, I Peter 1:7, I Peter 4:12–14.
53. I Thessalonians 5:18.
54. Philippians 4:4.
55. II Corinthians 12:10.
56. Matthew 5:11–12.
57. Isaiah 61:1.
58. Luke 4:17–19.
59. II Corinthians 12:9.
60. II Corinthians 12:10.
61. James 1:2–4.
62. I Peter 2:20–21.
63. I Peter 4:12–14.
64. I Peter 4:12–14, Hebrews 10:34.
65. Romans 8:18.
66. I Peter 4:14.
67. II Corinthians 3:18.
68. II Corinthians 4:6.
69. James Strong, S.T.D., LL.D, *Strong's Exhaustive Concordance of the Bible*, McDonald Publishing Company, McClean, Virginia, #1391.
70. Romans 8:18.
71. Romans 5:8.
72. John 16:13.
73. John 16:8.
74. Galatians 5:22.
75. I Corinthians 13:1.
76. I Peter 1:1–2.
77. Ephesians 3:7.
78. I Peter 1:22.
79. Acts 2:13.
80. Acts 2:22–23.
81. Acts 2:29.
82. II Timothy 1:7.
83. James Strong, S.T.D., LL.D, *Strong's Exhaustive Concordance of the Bible*, McDonald Publishing Company, McClean, Virginia, #4995.
84. John 14:12, 16.
85. Matthew 11:5.
86. Dwight L. Moody, *Secret Power,* Regal Books, Ventura, 1987, p. 17.
87. V. Raymond Edman, *They Found the Secret*, ZondervanPublishingHouse, Grand Rapids, 1960, p. 65.
88. Ibid., pp. 67–68.
89. Romans 8:16.
90. I Thessalonians 5:23.
91. Luke 11:13.
92. Ephesians 5:18.
93. Romans 6:13.
94. Galatians 5:16.
95. I Samuel 17:40.
96. II Corinthians 12:7–10.
97. James Strong, S.T.D., LL.D, *Strong's Exhaustive Concordance of the Bible*, McDonald Publishing Company, McClean, Virginia, #769.
98. II Corinthians 4:16.
99. James Strong, S.T.D., LL.D, *Strong's Exhaustive Concordance of the Bible*, McDonald Publishing Company, McClean, Virginia, #5196.

100. I Peter 3:9.
101. James Strong, S.T.D.,
     LL.D, *Strong's Exhaustive Concordance of the Bible*, McDonald Publishing Company, McClean, Virginia, *#4730.*
102. I Thessalonians 5:18.
103. Romans 5:2–5.
104. Exodus 16:8.
105. Ephesians 4:26–27.
106. Northwoods Conference Center, January 2000.
107. Luke 16:23–24.
108. James 3.
109. II Corinthians 12:9.

Truth without love brings reaction because God is love and God is truth. Therefore, sincere love is the strongest proof of genuine truth.

"But speaking the truth in love, may grow up into him in all things, which is the head, even Christ."

—Ephesians 4:15

Chapter
2

THE POWER OF ITS CONVERSIONS

Chapter Summary

*F*ollow-up programs among today's converts reveal that less than 10 percent continue on with serious Bible study or fellowship with a local church. In contrast, the three thousand new believers on the Day of Pentecost continued steadfastly in the faith. It is important for us to understand why they did so. First, since they were devout Jews, they had a thorough knowledge of the Scriptures. Second, they were given the truth of the Gospel in the power and love of the Holy Spirit. This power of love was transferred to the converts as evidenced by the amazing generosity they had toward each other. Third, they saw the relationship between persecution and receiving the power of the Spirit. Therefore, they did not survive *in spite of* persecutions; they thrived *because of* them.

METHODS OF SOUL WINNING

There is joy in Heaven over one sinner who repents,[1] and there is great joy among believers when they learn that someone has made a decision to receive Christ as their Savior.

The goal and emphasis in the Church during the second half of the twentieth century has been to bring people to the point of making a decision for Christ. Thousands have come to Christ in this way. However, those who have specialized in follow-up programs have reported a disturbing condition.

A high number of converts fail to complete any kind of Bible study course or become active in a local church after their decision. One ministry that specializes in following up on hundreds of thousands of converts reports that to discover as many as 10 percent of new converts who have taken further steps to get involved in growth as a Christian would be unusual. Other estimates range between 3 and 5 percent.[2]

Scripture records a far different response among those who were converted in the first century. "Then they that gladly received his word were baptized: and the same day there were added unto them about three thousand souls. And they continued stedfastly in the apostles' doctrine and fellowship, and in breaking of bread, and in prayers. . . . And they, continuing daily with one accord in the temple, and breaking bread from house to house, did eat their meat with gladness and singleness of heart."[3]

Notice that it does not state that 10 percent of them continued steadfastly, but rather that the vast majority, if not all of them, continued steadfastly in the apostles' doctrine, fellowship, the breaking of bread, and prayers.

Not only did they follow through on their decision, but their testimony caused multitudes to be added to the church.[4] They were zealous of good works and spread the Gospel wherever they went. Soon the entire world was impacted by their witness, as noted by their enemies: "These that have turned the world upside down are come hither also."[5]

First-century converts rejected earthly materialism[6] and smiled in the face of ridicule and rejection. They praised God for beatings and persecutions[7] and "took joyfully" the spoiling of their goods.[8]

What factors made the difference between first-century conversions and modern-day decisions?

1. THEY BASED THEIR FAITH ON THE WORD

The Scripture states, "Then they that gladly received his word were baptized."[9] The multitudes that were in Jerusalem on the Day of Pentecost were devout Jews and proselytes from many cities and nations. They had a thorough knowledge of Old Testament Scriptures, and were able to quickly understand the message of Peter when he quoted from these Scriptures.

Faith is necessary for salvation. In fact, we are saved by grace through faith,[10] and "faith cometh by hearing, and hearing by the word of God."[11] Jesus explained the falling away of believers in terms of their response to the Word of God.

"Behold, a sower went forth to sow; And when he sowed, some seeds fell by the way side, and the fowls came and devoured them up: Some fell upon stony places, where they had not much earth: and forthwith they sprung up, because they had no deepness of earth:

"And when the sun was up, they were scorched; and because they had no root, they withered away. And some fell among thorns; and the thorns sprung up, and choked them: But other fell into good ground, and brought forth fruit, some an hundredfold, some sixtyfold, some thirtyfold."[12]

Jesus then explained this parable. "When any one heareth the word of the kingdom, and understandeth it not, then cometh the wicked one, and catcheth away that which was sown in his heart. This is he which received seed by the way side.

"But he that received the seed into stony places, the same is he that heareth the word, and anon with joy receiveth it; Yet hath he not root in himself, but dureth for a while: for when tribulation or persecution ariseth because of the word, by and by he is offended.

"He also that received seed among the thorns is he that heareth the word; and the care of this world, and the deceitfulness of riches, choke the word, and he becometh unfruitful. But he that received seed into the good ground is he that heareth the word, and understandeth it; which also beareth fruit, and bringeth forth, some an hundredfold, some sixty, some thirty."[13]

The need for lasting decisions to be based on a clear understanding of the Word of God is powerfully illustrated in the case of the Ethiopian eunuch. He had the Scriptures, but could not understand them until Philip explained how they spoke of Jesus Christ and His death on the cross for him. When the Ethiopian eunuch understood the message, he eagerly believed on the Lord Jesus Christ and requested to be baptized.[14]

2. The Power of Love Was Transferred

The same power of the Holy Spirit that came "upon" the disciples in the upper room was transferred through their lives and message to the multitudes who heard them.

The love of those who were converted was so great that they sold their possessions and distributed the money to other believers and those in need.[15] Love is most effectively demonstrated through true generosity.[16]

An initial indicator of the love that was communicated on the Day of Pentecost was Peter's response to those who mocked him and said, "These men are full of new wine."[17]

Just a few weeks earlier, Peter might have reacted in anger or irritation. Now, however, he remembered and obeyed the teachings of Jesus Christ who said, "Blessed are ye, when men shall revile you, and persecute you, and shall say all manner of evil against you falsely, for my sake. Rejoice, and be exceeding glad: for great is your reward in heaven."[18]

Peter was rewarded with the conversion and transformation of three thousand people who, not too many weeks earlier, had demanded the death of Jesus Christ. He lovingly responded to their ridicule by pointing out why their accusation could not be true and then patiently explained what was actually happening.

The example and influence of Peter's love is also seen in the response by other believers to persecution, such as in the case of Stephen, when he was falsely accused in the council. Stephen correctly responded to the accusations and was filled with wisdom, joy, and love for all those present.

The power of Stephen's love was further demonstrated as he forgave the ones who were killing him. "And he kneeled down, and cried with a loud voice, Lord, lay not this sin to their charge. And when he had said this, he fell asleep."[19]

Stephen had good cause to rejoice in this martyrdom, because only eternity will reveal all of those who were brought to Christ through his death. Among them is the Apostle Paul, who was deeply impacted and whose incredible fruitfulness will be shared by Stephen throughout all eternity. "And when the blood of thy martyr Stephen was shed, I also was standing by, and consenting unto his death, and kept the raiment of them that slew him."[20]

The sequence of receiving more love through the power of the Holy Spirit, by properly responding to persecutions and tribulation, is clearly taught in Scripture.

"Therefore being justified by faith, we have peace with God through our Lord Jesus Christ: By whom also we have access by faith into this grace wherein we stand, and rejoice in hope of the glory of God. And not only so, but we glory in tribulations also: knowing that tribulation worketh patience; And patience, experience; and experience, hope: And hope maketh not ashamed; because the love of God is shed abroad in our hearts by the Holy Ghost which is given unto us."[21]

3. THE LAW WAS USED TO BRING CONVICTION

The goal of the Holy Spirit is to produce genuine brokenness and conviction in the heart of a sinner.[22] This is accomplished by bringing every person face to face with the holy Law of God.

The Apostle Paul explains how effective the Law is in bringing about conviction of sin. "I had not known sin, but by the law: for I had not known lust, except the law had said, Thou shalt not covet."[23] The shallowness of modern-day conversions is painfully described by the following account from Mr. Ray Comfort.

I received the following letter from a frustrated pastor in Florida. It's typical of what happens when evangelism doesn't follow the Biblical pattern:

"We have seen . . . over a thousand led to the Lord in the street's [sic] . . . I have been thinking about the follow up/involvement ratio here and it ain't [sic] great, rather it stinks . . . not many of these teens are at church.

"I've been analyzing this and last month for example I preached face to face on the streets the whole Gospel (death, burial, resurrection) with focus on repentance, and remission to 155 people, 70 made commitments to Christ. I know my preaching is correct, but I know I need better follow up. Any recommendation's [sic]?"

His dilemma was that he was preaching the light of the Gospel ("the death, burial, and resurrection"), without the use of the Law to awaken his hearers. Like many others who see this enigma, he thought that his converts needed more follow-up. However, to fall into the trap of thinking that follow-up will solve the problem, is like thinking that putting a stillborn child into intensive care will fix that problem.

He wasn't alone in his stillborn dilemma. The following statistics are extremely difficult to come by, as they are not exactly published with too much enthusiasm:

According to *Annual Church Ministries Report* (a publication of a major U.S. denomination of 11,500 churches), the combined Fellowship was able to obtain 294,784 decisions for Christ in 1991. However, they could only find 14,337 in fellowship. That means that they couldn't account for 280,000 of their decisions.[24]

"Three to sixteen percent of those who make decisions at crusades end up responsible members of a church . . . that's not counting Christians who recommit their lives."[25]

Church Growth Magazine reported that a mass crusade obtained 18,000 decisions for Christ, but that 94% failed to even become incorporated into local churches.[26]

Paul describes the Law as a schoolmaster that brings us to Christ. In Paul's day, a schoolmaster or "pedagogue" was not the teacher but a trusted slave who was a stern disciplinarian. He was responsible to take a child of nobility to the master teacher.[27]

In efforts to bring people to a decision for Christ, many well-meaning believers have assured non-Christians that if they receive Christ they will have a happier life. This is true only if tribulation, persecution, trials, temptations, and distresses can be defined as happiness.

These circumstances are actually sources of joy, when viewed as the means for receiving greater power from the Holy Spirit. Even as Jesus said, "Blessed are ye, when men shall revile you, and persecute you, and shall say all manner of evil against you falsely, for my sake. Rejoice, and be exceeding glad: for great is your reward in heaven."[28]

Most new believers are totally unprepared for trials and tribulations. Thus they become disillusioned with Christianity and turn their backs on it,[29] not realizing that the trials were designed to test their faith and obedience so that the power of the Holy Spirit may come upon them.

Charles Finney saw hundreds of thousands of people come to salvation as he presented the Law to them. Fifteen years after his ministry ended, a study was made of those who were converted under his preaching. It was discovered that 75 percent of them were still following the Lord and active in local churches.

Charles Finney did not ask for decisions for Christ; instead, he preached the Law of God and helped each one understand how he had broken God's Law and was on his way to an eternity of judgment. He explains this in his lectures on revival. His hearers would come under deep conviction and often cry out to God for mercy.

> Pains enough had not been taken to search the heart and thoroughly detect and expose the sinner's depravity, so as to make him see the need of the gospel remedy. If I am not mistaken, there has been, in many cases, an error committed in urging sinners to submission before they are prepared to understand what

true submission is. . . . to believe, before they have understood their need of Christ; to resolve to serve God, before they have at all understood what the service of God is. . . .

Consequently all his ideas of God, of sin, of his own guilt and desert of punishment, his need of a Savior, the necessity of his being saved from his sins—in short, every fundamental idea of the Christian religion is apprehended by him with very little clearness. His mind is dark; his heart is hard.

He has never been stripped of his self-dependence and self-righteousness; consequently, he has never known Christ, "the power of His resurrection, the fellowship of His sufferings," nor the "being made conformable unto his death";[30] nor has he even an idea of what these things mean. He knows little of Christ more than the name, and an obscure idea of His mediatorial work and relations. . . . He has no deep consciousness of sustaining the relation of an outlaw and a condemned criminal to the government of God, and being dead to all hope in himself or in any other creature.

In short, instead of seeing his necessities, his true character and relations, his views of all these things are so exceedingly superficial, that he has not apprehended, and does not apprehend, the necessity and nature of gospel salvation.[31]

This is not to say that a person cannot experience genuine salvation without a thorough understanding of the theological implications of salvation. Salvation is a gift of God through faith in the finished work of the Lord Jesus Christ. It is received by calling upon the Lord. "For whosoever shall call upon the name of the Lord shall be saved."[32] God gives children an extra measure of faith and states, "Except ye be converted, and become as little children, ye shall not enter into the kingdom of heaven."[33] God also writes His Law in their hearts. "Which shew the work of the law written in their hearts, their conscience also bearing witness, and their thoughts the mean while accusing or else excusing one another."[34]

The primary thrust of Peter's message was to prove through the Law and the prophets that Jesus was the anointed One of God, Whom they took and had by wicked hands crucified and slain.[35] "Now when they heard this, they were pricked in their heart, and said unto Peter and to the rest of the apostles, Men and brethren, what shall we do?"[36] Peter then told them to repent and be baptized.

4. THE APPEAL WAS MADE TO THE CONSCIENCE

The message of salvation can be designed to appeal to the mind, will, emotions, or conscience of an unbeliever.

Appealing to the mind or intellect seems logical on the basis that the Gospel is reasonable, which it is to a believer who has spiritual discernment. However, "the natural man receiveth not the things of the Spirit of God: for they are foolishness unto him: neither can he know them, because they are spiritually discerned."[37]

Appealing to the emotions can be done through "soul music;" however, when the emotions change, the decision may also change. Making an appeal to the will is done by urging one to make a decision, which is important but is not from the heart and can be temporary.

Appealing to the conscience, however, involves bringing a person to accept personal responsibility for his own actions. The entire multitude was cut to the heart as Peter proved from the Old Testament Scriptures that Jesus was the Christ. He declared, "Therefore let all the house of Israel know assuredly, that God hath made that same Jesus, whom ye have crucified, both Lord and Christ."[38]

Actually, every person in the world is responsible for the death of Jesus because "he was wounded for *our* transgressions, he was bruised for *our* iniquities: the chastisement of *our* peace was upon him; and with his stripes we are healed."[39] Therefore, Peter's message given on the Day of Pentecost is applicable to every person.

5. They "Called Out" for Salvation

It is commonly understood that salvation comes by "praying to receive Christ as Savior." Yet the Scripture repeatedly emphasizes that salvation is the result of a "call." Peter stated, "And it shall come to pass, that whosoever shall **call** on the name of the Lord shall be saved."[40]

Paul emphasized the same point: "For there is no difference between the Jew and the Greek: for the same Lord over all is rich unto all that **call** upon him. For whosoever shall **call** upon the name of the Lord shall be saved. How then shall they **call** on him in whom they have not believed? and how shall they believe in him of whom they have not heard? and how shall they hear without a preacher?"[41]

Scripture makes a clear distinction between a prayer and a call. Some of the many references are as follows.

"Hear my cry, O God; attend unto my prayer."[42] "Hearken unto the voice of my cry, my King, and my God: for unto thee will I pray."[43] "Hear the right, O LORD, attend unto my cry, give ear unto my prayer, that goeth not out of feigned lips."[44]

". . . Hearken unto the cry and to the prayer, which thy servant prayeth . . . ."[45] "Therefore pray not thou for this people, neither lift up a cry or prayer for them: for I will not hear them in the time that they cry unto me for their trouble."[46]

When Jesus was crucified, two other men were also crucified. One railed him; the other said, "Lord, remember me when thou comest into thy kingdom." Jesus responded by saying, "To-day shalt thou be with me in paradise."[47]

In the Temple, two men came before the Lord. One was a Pharisee who prayed a self-righteous prayer. The other man was a publican who did not so much as lift up his head but smote his chest and said, "God be merciful to me a sinner." Jesus responded, "I tell you, this man went down to his house justified rather than the other: for every one that exalteth himself shall be abased; and he that humbleth himself shall be exalted."[48]

The very purpose of a cry is to signify unconditional surrender and a conquering of pride. It is an acknowledgement of our helplessness and a plea for God's mercy. It is saying, "I am unworthy and cannot do it myself; God, you must do it."

This is not to say that one who prays to receive Christ will not be saved, because God looks at the heart. Yet the Biblical pattern involves "crying out" for the salvation of God.

6. THE NEED FOR BAPTISM WAS TAUGHT

After deep conviction upon hearing the truth, the multitude asked Peter and the rest of the apostles, "Men and brethren, what shall we do?"[49]

Peter emphasized the immediate need for them to repent, be baptized, and receive the Holy Spirit for the purpose of saving themselves from their evil and adulterous generation.[50]

Peter continued exhorting them "with many words" to claim the promise of the life that is in Christ Jesus for them and their children. There is little doubt that the "many words" included further teaching on the vital work of the Holy Spirit in their lives.

When Jesus came to be baptized by John at the River Jordan, John objected by stating that he himself needed Jesus' baptism. Yet Jesus replied, "Suffer it to be so now: for thus it becometh us to fulfil all righteousness."[51]

John had predicted the type of baptism that Jesus would give: "John answered, saying unto them all, I indeed baptize you with water; but one mightier than I cometh, the latchet of whose shoes I am not worthy to unloose: he shall baptize you with the Holy Ghost and with fire."[52]

• Baptism With Water

As previously stated, a person's spirit is born of the Holy Spirit when one calls upon the Lord to be saved.[53] Believers receive the Holy Spirit as they are born again through faith in Jesus Christ and become a part of His spiritual body.[54]

It was the power of the indwelling Holy Spirit, the power of love, that caused a remarkable bonding among believers in the first-century Church. That bond was strengthened by *water* baptism. "For by one Spirit are we all baptized into one body, whether we be Jews or Gentiles, whether we be bond or free; and have been all made to drink into one Spirit."[55]

The baptism with water is a baptism into Christ[56] for those who believe with all their hearts that Jesus is the Son of God.[57] He who believes should be baptized[58] to make that public proclamation of faith in Christ as his Lord and Savior.

A further bond came as the disciples realized that they were being baptized into the death of Christ and that they were identifying themselves with the power of his death, burial, and resurrection. "Know ye not, that so many of us as were baptized into Jesus Christ were baptized into his death? Therefore we are buried with him by baptism into death: that like as Christ was raised up from the dead by the glory of the Father, even so we also should walk in newness of life."[59]

If the focus of baptism with water is not on dying to oneself and rising to a new life in Christ, carnality about baptism can even develop within the church. In the Corinthian church, for example, believers developed a loyalty to the individual or group that baptized them rather than to the Body of Christ. Thus Paul stated, "Now this I say, that every one of you saith, I am of Paul; and I of Apollos; and I of Cephas; and I of Christ. Is Christ divided? was Paul crucified for you? or were ye baptized in the name of Paul? I thank God that I baptized none of you, but Crispus and Gaius; Lest any should say that I had baptized in mine own name."[60]

• Baptism With the Holy Ghost

The mark of a true believer in Christ is the indwelling Holy Spirit,[61] but the Holy Spirit's role is not limited to renewing our spirit.

He also gives us power to overcome sin,[62] leads us in all truth,[63] comforts us in time of need,[64] and renews our minds.[65] That is why we are commanded to be filled with the Spirit[66] and not to grieve[67] or quench[68] the Holy Spirit.

Every believer should desire as much of the Holy Spirit in his or her life as God permits. The Holy Spirit is our source of love, joy, peace, long-suffering, gentleness, goodness, and faith.[69]

Our Heavenly Father desires to give His children the Holy Spirit.[70] In fact, this was the reason Jesus came. John said that Jesus would baptize with the Holy Ghost and with fire.[71]

The same power that clothed the disciples and gave them the love for ministry was available to the multitude, based upon the promise of God: "For the promise is unto you, and to your children, and to all that are afar off, even as many as the Lord our God shall call."[72]

When a person is truly repentant and calls upon the Lord for salvation, he should be told about the One Who will be guiding him in the truth of Scripture and helping him in his daily walk. He should know that the Holy Spirit will confirm with his spirit that he is a Christian and that he himself must ask his Heavenly Father to fill his soul with the Holy Spirit. It is then the believer's responsibility to yield his body to the control of the Holy Spirit.

• Baptism With Fire

A new believer should also be informed that there is a further endowment of power by the Holy Spirit which will produce a wonderful overflow of love in his life for service unto the Lord. However, to experience this, he must joyfully welcome trials and temptations. Those who overcome receive crowns and rewards. Therefore we are instructed, "Let us not be weary in well-doing: for in due season we shall reap, if we faint not."[73]

John's reference to the baptism with fire also refers to a coming day of judgment. However, it is significant that on the Day of Pentecost, cloven tongues of fire were upon each disciple that received the power of the Holy Spirit.[74]

The baptism with fire is also consistent with the fiery trial that every believer will be led into by the Holy Spirit after salvation. "Beloved, think it not strange concerning the fiery trial which is to try you, as though some strange thing happened unto you."[75]

In Scripture we are told of fiery trials and fiery judgments. The purpose of a fiery trial is to purify our faith. "That the trial of your faith, being much more precious than of gold that perisheth, though it be tried with fire, might be found unto praise and honour and glory at the appearing of Jesus Christ."[76]

As we give thanks and rejoice in the Lord during the baptisms with fire, we are endued with more power of the Holy Spirit—the power of love.

Notes

1. Luke 15:7.
2. *American Horizon*, Editoral—March/April 1993.
3. Acts 2:41–42, 46.
4. Acts 5:14.
5. Acts 17:6.
6. Acts 4:34–35.
7. Acts 5:40–41.
8. Hebrews 10:34.
9. Acts 2:41.
10. Ephesians 2:8.
11. Romans 10:17.
12. Matthew 13:3–8.
13. Matthew 13:19–23.
14. Acts 8:26–38.
15. Acts 2:45.
16. John 3:16.
17. Acts 2:13.
18. Matthew 5:11–12.
19. Acts 7:60.
20. Acts 22:20.
21. Romans 5:1–5.
22. John 16:8.
23. Romans 7:7.
24. *American Horizon*, Editorial—March/April 1993, p. 3.
25. *Southern California Christian Times*, July 1993.
26. *God Loves You and Has a Wonderful Plan for Your Life—the fallacy of the modern message* by Ray Comfort.
27. Galatians 3:24.
28. Matthew 5:11–12.
29. Mark 4:19.
30. Philippians 3:10.
31. Charles G. Finney, "Letter III. A Cause of Spurious Conversions," *Revival Fire*, Metropolitan Church Association, Waukesha, Wisconsin, pp. 18–20.
32. Romans 10:13.
33. Matthew 18:3.
34. Romans 2:15.
35. Acts 2:23.
36. Acts 2:37.
37. I Corinthians 2:14.
38. Acts 2:36.
39. Isaiah 53:5, emphasis added.
40. Acts 2:21, emphasis added.
41. Romans 10:12–14, emphasis added.
42. Psalm 61:1.
43. Psalm 5:2.
44. Psalm 17:1.
45. I Kings 8:28.
46. Jeremiah 11:14.
47. Luke 23:39–43.
48. Luke 18:10–14.
49. Acts 2:37.
50. Acts 2:38–40.
51. Matthew 3:15.
52. Luke 3:16.
53. John 3:5, Romans 10:13.
54. Romans 8:14–16.
55. I Corinthians 12:13.
56. Galatians 3:26–27.
57. Acts 8:36–37.
58. Mark 16:16, Acts 2:38.
59. Romans 6:3–4.
60. I Corinthians 1:12–15.
61. Ephesians 1:13.
62. Romans 8:13.
63. John 16:13.
64. John 16:7.
65. Romans 12:2.
66. Ephesians 5:18.
67. Ephesians 4:30.
68. I Thessalonians 5:19.
69. Galatians 5:22.
70. Luke 11:13.
71. Matthew 3:11, Mark 1:8, Luke 3:16, John 1:33, John 7:37–38, Acts 11:14–16, Acts 1:5.
72. Acts 2:39.
73. Galatians 6:9.
74. Acts 2:3.
75. I Peter 4:12.
76. I Peter 1:7.

The more confident we are of our answers, the more commitment we can require of our hearers.

―――――――――――

"Then said Jesus unto his disciples, If any man will come after me, let him deny himself, and take up his cross, and follow me."

―*Matthew 16:24*

Chapter

3

The Power of Its Teachings

Chapter Summary

*W*hat teaching could be so powerful that it commanded the "steadfast" commitment of all the believers? What training could be so effective that it equipped believers to be powerful witnesses of their faith and to be joyful in the face of temptations, trials, and persecutions? The answer is found in the "apostles' doctrine," which contained the authority and power of the doctrine of Christ, the rich wisdom of the Old Testament, and the dynamic new revelation given by the Holy Spirit and eventually written out in the New Testament. All who heard these teachings were astonished and the lives of those who followed them were transformed. These teachings were part of a kingdom message with character instruction for all people of all times.

The Meaning of the Apostles' Doctrine

The phrase "the apostles' doctrine" is used only once in the New Testament. It defines the teaching that the apostles gave to the multitudes of new believers after the Day of Pentecost.[1]

The word *doctrine* comes from the Greek word *didache* meaning "instruction" or teaching.[2] What was the teaching that the apostles gave to the new believers?

It is obvious that the teaching which the apostles gave came from the three years of training they had just received from the Lord Jesus Christ. In His teaching, He gave the true intent of the Old Testament Scriptures, which was true holiness based on loving God and loving your neighbor as yourself.[3] He also explained how all Old Testament Scriptures referred to Him and His ministry.

On the road to Emmaus, the disciples marveled as Jesus began with Moses and the prophets and explained Himself. Later, they recalled, "Did not our heart burn within us, while he talked with us by the way, and while he opened to us the scriptures?"[4]

All additional training that the apostles gave was based on Christ's own words and on principles that led to Christlike living.[5] This further revelation, inspired by the Holy Spirit, was written in the books of the New Testament.[6]

THE CONTENT OF THE APOSTLES' DOCTRINE

The last instruction Jesus gave to his disciples was to go into all the world and teach all the truths that He had taught them, "teaching them to observe all things whatsoever I have commanded you: and, lo, I am with you alway, even unto the end of the world. Amen."[7]

What then was the basic content of the teachings of Jesus, also referred to in Scripture as the doctrine of Christ? "Whosoever transgresseth, and abideth not in the doctrine of Christ, hath not God. He that abideth in the doctrine of Christ, he hath both the Father and the Son."[8]

The teachings of Jesus are clearly stated in His Sermon on the Mount (Matthew 5–7). Those who heard the powerful truths from these three chapters were astonished, because these teachings were so different from what they were accustomed to hearing from the scribes and Pharisees.

"And it came to pass, when Jesus had ended these sayings, the people were astonished at his doctrine: For he taught them as one having authority, and not as the scribes."[9] There was astonishment whenever and wherever He repeated this doctrine.

When Jesus taught in the synagogue, "they were astonished at his doctrine: for he taught them as one that had authority."[10] Those who heard Him teach in Capernaum "were astonished at his doctrine: for his word was with power."[11]

Jesus explained that His doctrine was really not His own; it was given to Him directly by His Father and would also be revealed to those who would do His will. "Jesus answered them, and said, My doctrine is not mine, but his that sent me. If any man will do his will, he shall know of the doctrine, whether it be of God, or whether I speak of myself."[12]

What then were the major themes of the doctrine of Christ that had such authority and power over those who heard them?

1. THE MESSAGE OF THE KINGDOM

Jesus began His discourse by talking about the kingdom. "Blessed are the poor in spirit: for theirs is the kingdom of heaven."[13] He taught us to pray, "Thy kingdom come. Thy will be done in earth, as it is in heaven. . . . For thine is the kingdom, and the power, and the glory, for ever. Amen."[14]

Jesus explained who would be the greatest and the least in the kingdom,[15] and He also gave the clear command: "But seek ye first the kingdom of God, and his righteousness; and all these things shall be added unto you."[16]

There are about one hundred and fifty references to the kingdom throughout the New Testament, which indicates its vital place in the teachings of Jesus and the apostles, including Paul.

The teachings about the kingdom of God have not been prevalent in recent years. In fact, some even assign this vital truth to some future age.

It is true that Christ's full and eternal kingdom will be established at the end of this age. Meanwhile, His present kingdom is to be experienced in the hearts and lives of all those who believe on Him for salvation. Even as Jesus said, "Behold, the kingdom of God is within you."[17]

Peter speaks of the eternal kingdom: "For so an entrance shall be ministered unto you abundantly into the everlasting kingdom of our Lord and Saviour Jesus Christ."[18]

However, John also spoke of a present kingdom: "I John, who also am your brother, and companion in tribulation, and in the kingdom and patience of Jesus Christ, was in the isle that is called Patmos, for the word of God, and for the testimony of Jesus Christ."[19]

If the kingdom message was only for the nation of Israel, as some suggest, then it certainly would not have been a major topic in the teachings of Paul, who was the apostle to the Gentiles. Paul both explains and continually emphasizes the kingdom message as the motivation for Godly living.

"Giving thanks unto the Father, which hath made us meet to be partakers of the inheritance of the saints in light: Who hath delivered us from the power of darkness, and hath translated us into the kingdom of his dear Son."[20]

A kingdom is composed of three elements: a king, the laws of the king, and citizens who are to obey those laws. The citizens of a kingdom will have their rewarding heritage in direct proportion to the power and riches of their king. The kingdom of God is "righteousness, and peace, and joy in the Holy Ghost."[21]

Those who obey the laws of God's kingdom not only enjoy this inheritance but also experience the mighty power of love and truth by the anointing of the Holy Spirit, "for the kingdom of God is not in word, but in power."[22]

Those who violate God's laws are like citizens who commit crimes. They are still citizens, but they lose certain rights and privileges that they otherwise would have enjoyed. They are like the Israelites in the wilderness who lusted after evil pleasures and turned away from God. God gave them the desires of their heart but sent leanness into their souls.[23]

Paul combined the teachings of the grace of God with the message of the kingdom of God when he spoke to the elders of the church of Ephesus: "I have received of the Lord Jesus, to testify the gospel of the grace of God. And now, behold, I know that ye all, among whom I have gone preaching the kingdom of God, shall see my face no more."[24]

Up to the end of his life, Paul preached the kingdom message. "And when they had appointed him a day, there came many to him into his lodging; to whom he expounded and testified the kingdom of God, persuading them concerning

Jesus, both out of the law of Moses, and out of the prophets, from morning till evening . . . . Preaching the kingdom of God, and teaching those things which concern the Lord Jesus Christ, with all confidence, no man forbidding him."[25]

Paul was not alone in his preaching of the kingdom to the early Church. "But when they believed Philip preaching the things concerning the kingdom of God, and the name of Jesus Christ, they were baptized, both men and women."[26]

Becoming Worthy of God's Kingdom

Paul gave a significant challenge to the Thessalonian Christians when he said, "That ye may be counted worthy of the kingdom of God, for which ye also suffer."[27] In previous verses, he praised them for their growing faith and their abounding love toward each other. Then he identified the source of their spiritual power—their patience and faith in all the persecutions and tribulations that they endured.[28]

The apostles trained new believers to not just endure persecution and tribulation, but to rejoice in it and thrive because of it. New believers understood that they were called to suffer because Christ suffered for them, leaving them an example, that they should follow in His steps.[29]

Paul affirmed both this calling and its purpose to produce the power of God. "Wherefore also we pray always for you, that our God would count you worthy of this calling, and fulfil all the good pleasure of his goodness, and the work of faith with power."[30]

Paul reminds the Thessalonian Christians in his first epistle that his message came to them, not in word only "but also in power, and in the Holy

The Kingdom Message on Power

The Indwelling of the Spirit	The Testing of the Spirit	The Power of the Spirit
1. Jesus was filled with the Spirit at baptism.	He was led by the Spirit into the wilderness.	He returned in the power of the Spirit for ministry.[34]
2. Jesus breathed upon the disciples and they received the Holy Spirit after Christ's resurrection.[35]	They were to wait in Jerusalem until they received power.[36]	The Holy Spirit came upon them at Pentecost in power for public ministry.[37]
3. Paul was filled with the Spirit when he received his sight after Ananias prayed for him.[38]	Paul suffered much persecution.[39]	Paul received the power of God's Spirit after tests and tribulations.[40]
4. A believer's spirit is born of the Holy Spirit at conversion,[41] and one's soul is filled with the Spirit by asking for it.[42]	All believers are to rejoice in tribulation. All that live Godly shall suffer persecution.[43]	"To comprehend with all saints . . . the love of Christ . . . according to the power that worketh in us."[44]

Ghost,"[31] and that the Thessalonian believers "received the word in much affliction, with joy of the Holy Ghost: So that ye were ensamples to all that believe."[32] Paul then explained that the fruit he bore in Thessalonica was a direct result of the sufferings and shameful treatment he had received before coming to them.[33]

2. THE MESSAGE OF CHARACTER

The laws of God's kingdom are all summarized in two basic commandments: "Thou shalt love the Lord thy God with all thy heart, and with all thy soul, and with all thy mind. This is the first and great commandment. And the second is like unto it, Thou shalt love thy neighbour as thyself. On these two commandments hang all the law and the prophets."[45]

Jesus began His kingdom message with eight character qualities that must be demonstrated in order for the citizens of His kingdom to be in harmony with the King and demonstrate genuine love to God and others. Defining love in terms of specific character qualities is essential because people have different perceptions of what love is. One person may think that certain actions demonstrate love, while another person will view those actions as expressions of unkindness, selfishness, or insensitivity.

Jesus is the ultimate personification of all good character. He is love, truth, kindness, patience, gentleness, and meekness. It is significant that Jesus described Himself in terms of character qualities. "Take my yoke upon you, and learn of me; for I am meek and lowly in heart: and ye shall find rest unto your souls."[46]

Jesus is the "express image" of His Father, "who being the brightness of his glory, and the express image of his person, and upholding all things by the word of his power, when he had by himself purged our sins, sat down on the right hand of the Majesty on high."[47]

The word *express* in this passage is significant. It is the Greek word *charakter* which depicts an engraver with the tool, engraving an exact copy or representation of the same character.[48]

All events in a believer's life can be understood and appreciated in terms of the specific character qualities that they are intended to produce if one responds to them properly. This is the promise of Scripture.

"And we know that all things work together for good to them that love God, to them who are the called according to his purpose. For whom he did foreknow, he also did predestinate to be conformed to the image of his Son, that he might be the firstborn among many brethren."[49]

Each of the beatitudes that Jesus identified in His kingdom message can be further defined by various character aspects of that beatitude.

1. Blessed Are the Poor in Spirit

To be poor in spirit is to have the outlook and attitude of a beggar—one who realizes he is nothing and has nothing, so he has nothing to lose. He looks instead to those outside of himself for necessary provisions.

From this attitude, the following character qualities will result:

- **Humility**—Recognizing my total unworthiness and need for God's mercy and daily provision

- **Alertness**—A beggar is alert to those who pass by. Blind Bartimaeus was alert to Jesus,[50] and the lame man was alert to Peter and John.[51]

- **Gratefulness**—Recognizing that everything I have and enjoy was given by God and others

- **Thriftiness**—Everything given to a beggar is precious and carefully used, not squandered.

2. Blessed Are They That Mourn

To mourn is to grieve over our sin and the iniquities that have separated us from fellowship with God. Mourning is part of the process of true repentance and reconciliation with God. It is letting God break my heart with the things that break His heart. Such an attitude is directly related to the following character qualities:

- **Reverence**—An awareness of being in the presence of a holy God and honoring His right to rule and establish laws for us to obey

- **Responsibility**—Being personally accountable for all my thoughts, words, actions, and attitudes

- **Thoroughness**—Carefully reviewing every aspect of my life in the light of God's Word and Spirit

- **Sincerity**—Exposing hypocrisy and realizing that integrity is being inwardly what people see or perceive me to be outwardly

- **Discretion**—Confessing faults and making restitution in a proper and appropriate manner

3. Blessed Are the Meek

The word *meekness* is often associated with *weakness*, yet the attitude of meekness is just the opposite. The true meaning of meekness is "my strength under God's control," and it is this quality that Jesus demonstrated when he made a whip and drove the money changers out of the Temple.[52] Meekness is yielding my personal rights to God and thanking Him for whatever He does with them. The following qualities are essential to this attitude:

- **Obedience**—The strength of a horse is of no value until it is under the control of its rider.

- **Contentment**—Meekness is realizing that the basic essentials of food and clothing are all I really need and then enjoying anything beyond this as abundance from the Lord.

- **Flexibility**—Not setting my affections on plans or goals that could be changed by those I serve

- **Deference**—Limiting my freedoms in order not to offend the tastes or wishes of others

4. Blessed Are Those Who Hunger and Thirst After Righteousness

Hunger is a natural and forceful drive that can be satisfied in ways that are beneficial or destructive. By longing after the character of God and the ways of the Christian life, we will experience true success and fulfillment. Several qualities that enhance this attitude are these:

- **Initiative**—Taking practical steps to seek the Lord through prayer, fasting, and His Word

- **Attentiveness**—Training our spiritual ears to hear the true meanings of God's way of life

- **Diligence**—Spending time and energy to study the Scriptures in order to understand the truth

- **Punctuality**—Being faithful to the appointed times of meeting with the Lord in His Word

- **Orderliness**—Arranging my schedule and possessions to eliminate unnecessary distractions

- **Virtue**—The Godly influence we have on others because of rightly responding to past failures

5. Blessed Are the Merciful

An attitude of mercy is in harmony with the character of God, because He is merciful, and "his mercy endureth for ever."[53] Mercy rejoices over justice but is neither appreciated nor understood until the requirements of justice are established and accepted. The following qualities are key to developing an attitude of mercy:

- **Sensitivity**—Being aware of the hopes and hurts of others, especially those who are offenders
- **Compassion**—Entering into the emotions of others by feeling their pain and sharing their sorrows
- **Forgiveness**—Conquering bitterness by emotionally releasing an offender and seeing benefits from the consequences of his offenses
- **Kindness**—Looking for ways to share practical benefits, especially those who have wronged me
- **Hospitality**—Opening my heart and resources to those who are in need of them

6. Blessed Are the Pure in Heart

To be pure in heart toward the Lord is to be free from the contaminations of the world that distract us and choke out the things of God. A pure heart is related to a single focus, based on the instruction in James: "Purify your hearts, ye double-minded."[54] These qualities are vital:

- **Discernment**—Recognizing hidden motives that compete against the purity of God's ways
- **Justice**—Aligning my life with the holy standards of God's Law, and judging all things by it
- **Truthfulness**—Being honest before God and others about the true condition of my heart and actions

7. Blessed Are the Peacemakers

When the first six attitudes are controlling our motives and actions, others will be attracted to the light of our lives and ask of us a reason for the hope that lies within us. Because of what we have learned in the process of developing these attitudes, we will be able to help them make peace with God and others. In order to do this, it is important to develop the following character qualities:

- **Availability**—Setting aside personal schedules and pleasures to have more time to help others
- **Wisdom**—Seeing the problems and difficulties of life from God's perspective rather than our own
- **Creativity**—Finding new and more effective ways to accomplish established goals and solutions
- **Persuasiveness**—Guiding important truths around another person's mental roadblocks
- **Resourcefulness**—Finding resources that others have overlooked or discarded, to meet needs
- **Cautiousness**—Realizing that some people are not open to the truth and will react to those who try to reveal the truth to them

8. Blessed Are Those Who Are Persecuted

A persecutor is one who stalks another and does all he can to make another's life miserable. He is a messenger of Satan to hinder, discourage, and defame a peacemaker. However, Paul lists persecution as one of the five ways that we gain the power of the Holy Spirit.[55] With this power, the Holy Spirit is able to accomplish peacemaking through us so that people are won to Christ and broken relationships are restored.

Both winning people to Christ and restoring broken relationships produce eternal rewards that far outweigh any persecution. Therefore, Jesus said, "Blessed are ye, when men shall revile you, and persecute you, and shall say all manner of evil against you falsely, for my sake. Rejoice, and be exceeding glad: for great is your reward in heaven."[56]

To prepare for this attitude, the following qualities are necessary:

- **Boldness**—Having no fear of death and knowing what I have to say and do is right in God's sight

- **Joyfulness**—The inward light and outward brightness of one who is rejoicing in all things

- **Endurance**—The inward strength to withstand trials and tribulations in order to finish the course and receive the eternal prize of God's "Well done!"

- **Faith**—Understanding from the *rhemas* of God's Word what He wants to accomplish in my life

- **Self-Control**—Establishing inward disciplines in order not to disqualify myself for eternal crowns

- **Patience**—Accepting difficult situations from God without giving Him a deadline to remove them

- **Dependability**—Fulfilling what I consented to do, even if it means unexpected sacrifice

- **Decisiveness**—Basing decisions on Biblical principles and standards, regardless of the results

- **Loyalty**—Using difficult times to demonstrate my commitment to God and those whom He has called me to serve

- **Determination**—Purposing to accomplish God's goals in God's time, regardless of the opposition

- **Gentleness**—Responding in love and concern to those who reject the truth and react to me

- **Enthusiasm**—The dynamic energy that results from knowing that the testing in this life will produce a great and eternal reward

THE APPLICATION OF CHARACTER

After establishing the foundational attitudes that are required for the citizens of God's kingdom, Jesus gives a powerful series of teachings on how to apply them in daily living.[57] Each one amplifies specific character qualities.

☐ **"Ye are the salt of the earth."**
Virtue is required to retard evil in the world.

☐ **"Ye are the light of the world."**
The brightness of joy and the kindness of good works prepare others to hear the truth.

☐ **"Exceed the Pharisees' righteousness."**
Requires sincerity, humility, and meekness

☐ **"Whosoever is angry with his brother"**
Requires forgiveness and compassion

☐ **"If thy brother hath ought against thee"**
Take initiative and be humble and diligent to ask forgiveness and make restitution.

☐ **"Whoso looketh upon a woman to lust"**
A motivation to be self-controlled rather than to pluck out the eye or cut off the hand

☐ **"Whosoever shall put away his wife"**
A call for loyalty and responsibility

☐ **"Let your yea be yea, and nay be nay."**
The application of sincerity and truthfulness

☐ **"Go with him a second mile."**
The second-mile concept requires obedience, faith, humility, and enthusiasm.

☐ **"Love your enemies."**—Requires wisdom
"Bless those who curse."—Show gratefulness.
"Do good to haters."—Use discernment.
"Pray for persecuters."—Demonstrate patience.

☐ **"Love and salute strangers."**
This will express initiative and kindness.

☐ **"Do thine alms secretly."**
Doing good works without recognition requires faith, humility, and meekness.

☐ **"Enter into thy closet to pray."**
Secret prayer is based on attentiveness, dependability, and reverence for a living God.

☐ **"Forgive your offenders."**
An expression of compassion and kindness

☐ **"Fast in secret."**
This will build self-control, endurance, discernment, and spiritual sensitivity.

☐ **"Lay up treasures in heaven."**
This requires faith, decisiveness, and thriftiness.

☐ **"No man can serve two masters."**
This demands contentment and decisiveness.

☐ **"Take no thought for tomorrow."**
This is an exercise in contentment, security, and faith.

☐ **"Seek first the kingdom of God."**
A heart that seeks after God will grow in discernment, wisdom, and diligence.

☐ **"Judge not, that ye be not judged."**
Judging comes from a lack of compassion.

☐ **"Cast out the beam in thine own eye."**
This action will take humility and discernment.

☐ **"Give not that which is holy unto dogs."**
The qualities of cautiousness and discernment are required to know when to give.

☐ **"Ask and it shall be given unto you."**
Making requests takes initiative and wisdom.

☐ **"Do to others as you want them to do to you."**
This calls for deference and patience.

☐ **"Enter ye into the straight gate."**
Responsibility and diligence are required.

☐ **"Beware of false prophets."**
Dealing with them involves discernment and cautiousness.

☐ **"Do the will of my Father in heaven."**
A call for obedience and endurance

☐ **"Build your house on the rock."**
Building requires initiative, wisdom, diligence, determination, and endurance.

In the same way that all character qualities are specific aspects of genuine love, so the entire Old Testament gives detailed instruction on how to more effectively love God and others. This is the message that impacted the disciples and all those who were won to Christ through the powerful witness of their lives and message.

Character is also the theme throughout the rest of the New Testament, such as this instruction: "Be ye kind one to another, tenderhearted, forgiving one another, even as God for Christ's sake hath forgiven you."

"Be ye therefore followers of God, as dear children; And walk in love, as Christ also hath loved us, and hath given himself for us."[58]

THE SIGNIFICANCE OF DOCTRINE FIRST

When God gives a list in Scripture, it is significant. Often the last point is the most important item on the list. An example of this is the list in I Corinthians 13: "Now abideth faith, hope, charity, these three; but the greatest of these is charity."[59]

The same sequence is followed and expanded by Peter. "Add to your faith virtue; and to virtue knowledge; And to knowledge temperance; and to temperance patience; and to patience godliness; And to godliness brotherly kindness; and to brotherly kindness charity."[60]

In the same way, the sequence of the list given in Acts 2:42 has special importance. "And they continued stedfastly in the apostles' doctrine and fellowship, and in breaking of bread, and in prayers."

The apostles' doctrine is the foundation of the discipleship of believers. Fellowship is to be built around the truth of that doctrine because how "can two walk together, except they be agreed?"[61] Also, how can light have fellowship with darkness? "But if we walk in the light, as he is in the light, we have fellowship one with another."[62]

The third item on the list is the communion table. This is essential in order to maintain purity of doctrine and genuineness of fellowship. Unconfessed sin brings spiritual darkness and doctrinal error because "the things of the Spirit . . . are spiritually discerned."[63] If fellowship has been broken by offenses, both the offender and the one offended are instructed by Scripture to initiate restoration, and this is to be done before communion is taken.[64]

The first three items, however, are essential for the fourth and most important activity on the list—effectual, fervent prayer. When believers are in one place and in one accord, there is power in their prayers. A further evidence of the importance of this fourth item is the name that Jesus has chosen for His Church. "It is written, My house shall be called the house of prayer."[65]

By starting with the apostles' doctrine, all the believers are able to grow spiritually, increase their faith, and examine their lives in accordance with Biblical truth. Rich fellowship, effective communion, and powerful prayer will all naturally flow from sound doctrine.

In the early years of the Basic Seminar, I asked a pastor of a large church if his facilities could be used for the weeklong Seminar. He and his board agreed. On the first night, He stood at the front of the auditorium as the doors were opened, one hour before the Seminar began. He watched in amazement as hundreds of young people and adults rushed down the aisles to get front seats.

When the pastor welcomed all who came, he said, "I have already learned a very important lesson at this Seminar. Every Sunday morning people come in the church and seek out the back seats. Tonight you came in and rushed for the front seats. From now on, I am not going to give any more sermons—I am going to call them seminars."

This was intended to be humorous and the people received it as such. However, the pastor probably did not understand what caused the people to rush for the front seats. They were not coming for entertainment, but for three hours of instruction on the apostles' doctrine.[66]

The entire Seminar message has been built on Christ's teaching of the Sermon on the Mount and the related truths of the New and Old Testaments. Whenever these truths are presented, they have authority and power.[67]

Recently I was given a videotaped message of one who spoke at a large convention. As the speaker began, I was impressed with his humility but wondered what he could say that would impact the large audience.

After an hour and a half of listening to every word he said, I and one hundred other people watching with me could have no other response but to go to our knees in prayer and deep soul searching. I do not ever recall seeing such a powerful response to a video message.

What was that message? The speaker simply quoted the entire Sermon on the Mount and then emphasized key points in the Sermon through personal application.[68]

Notes

1. Acts 2:42.
2. James Strong, S.T.D., LL.D, *Strong's Exhaustive Concordance of the Bible*, McDonald Publishing Company, McClean, Virginia, *#1322*.
3. Matthew 22:37–39.
4. Luke 24:32.
5. I Timothy 6:3.
6. John 16:13.
7. Matthew 28:20.
8. II John 9.
9. Matthew 7:28–29.
10. Mark 1:22.
11. Luke 4:32.
12. John 7:16–17.
13. Matthew 5:3.
14. Matthew 6:10, 13.
15. Matthew 18:1, 4.
16. Matthew 6:33.
17. Luke 17:21.
18. II Peter 1:11.
19. Revelation 1:9.
20. Colossians 1:12–13.
21. Romans 14:17.
22. I Corinthians 4:20.
23. Psalm 106:15.
24. Acts 20:24–25.
25. Acts 28:23, 31.
26. Acts 8:12.
27. II Thessalonians 1:5.
28. II Thessalonians 1:3–4.
29. I Peter 2:21, I Peter 4:1, Philippians 1:29.
30. II Thessalonians 1:11–12.
31. I Thessalonians 1:5.
32. I Thessalonians 1:6–7.
33. I Thessalonians 2:2, II Corinthians 12:9–10.
34. Luke 4:1–14.
35. John 20:22.
36. Acts 1:4.
37. Acts 1:8–2:19.
38. Acts 9:17–18.
39. Acts 9:16.
40. II Corinthians 12:9–11.
41. John 3:5.
42. Luke 11:13.
43. Matthew 5:10–20, II Timothy 3:12, Philippians 4:4, I Thessalonians 5:18.
44. Ephesians 3:18–20, Acts 7:54–60.
45. Matthew 22:37–40.
46. Matthew 11:29.
47. Hebrews 1:3.
48. James Strong, S.T.D., LL.D, *Strong's Exhaustive Concordance of the Bible*, McDonald Publishing Company, McClean, Virginia, *#5481*.
49. Romans 8:28–29.
50. Mark 10:46–47.
51. Acts 3:1–3.
52. John 2:15.
53. Psalm 118:1.
54. James 4:8.
55. II Corinthians 12:9–10.
56. Matthew 5:11–12.
57. Matthew 5–7.
58. Ephesians 4:32–5:2.
59. I Corinthians 13:13.
60. II Peter 1:5–7.
61. Amos 3:3.
62. I John 1:7.
63. I Corinthians 2:14.
64. Matthew 5:23–24, Matthew 18:15.
65. Matthew 21:13.
66. Pastor of First Baptist Church, Elmhurst.
67. Matthew 7:29.
68. Rev. Keith Daniel, "Christ's Cry to the Church of This Day and Age," Heart-Cry for Revival Conference, Lancaster, Pennsylvania.

Fellowship takes place when two or more people are on the same side of a struggle.

"That I may know him, and the power of his resurrection, and the fellowship of his sufferings, being made conformable unto his death."

—*Philippians 3:10*

Chapter

4

THE POWER OF ITS FELLOWSHIP

Chapter Summary

The fellowship of first-century believers grew out of their commitment to the apostles' doctrine and their application of its truths to their daily lives. As they gave personal testimonies, believers were edified, financial needs were met, and a powerful spirit of love was experienced by everyone. The physical and spiritual rewards of their fellowship bonded the group together. The most severe form of church discipline was the separation and shunning of an erring member.

THE BASIS OF MEMBERSHIP

The fellowship of the first-century Church was so dynamic that it transformed the way believers thought, lived, and used their resources of time and money. It bonded together all those who were genuine believers and exposed those who were not a part of the Body of Christ. "And of the rest durst no man join himself to them: but the people magnified them."[1]

John wrote of those who were in the company of believers but were inwardly against Christ: "They went out from us, but they were not of us; for if they had been of us, they would no doubt have continued with us: but they went out, that they might be made manifest that they were not all of us."[2]

John then identified the distinguishing factor between those who were part of the fellowship and those who were not: "But ye have an unction from the Holy One, and ye know all things."[3] The Greek word for *unction* is *chrisma*.[4] It means "the special endowment ('chrism') of the Holy Spirit:—anointing."

THE EFFECTIVENESS OF DISCIPLINE

The daily fellowship of all the believers was so essential and valuable that the ultimate church discipline was simply to be disallowed from it.[5] Such discipline brought sorrow, remorse, and repentance to the immoral believer in the Corinthian church. After the man who committed fornication repented, Paul instructed the church to forgive, comfort, and restore him to their fellowship "lest perhaps such a one should be swallowed up with overmuch sorrow."[6]

THE MEANS OF MUTUAL EDIFICATION

There are many aspects of true fellowship among believers; however, the ultimate purpose is to edify one another so that each believer can come to full maturity and a unity in faith. For this purpose also, God gave to the Church apostles, prophets, evangelists, pastors, and teachers "for the perfecting of the saints, for the work of the ministry, for the edifying of the body of Christ."[7]

The primary purpose for the fellowship among believers is explained by Paul. "And let us consider one another to provoke unto love and to good works: Not forsaking the assembling of ourselves together, as the manner of some is; but exhorting one another: and so much the more, as ye see the day approaching."[8]

TWENTY-FIVE "ONE ANOTHER" COMMANDS

The interaction that believers are to have with each other is extensive. There are twenty-five different commands that God gives which are to be carried out among all believers.

1. Love one another. (This command is repeated twelve times in Scripture.)[9]
2. Be kindly affectioned one to another.[10]
3. Prefer one another in honor.[11]
4. Be of the same mind one toward another.[12]
5. Edify one another.[13]
6. Receive one another as Christ received us.[14]
7. Admonish one another.[15]
8. Greet one another.[16]
9. Serve one another.[17]
10. Forbear one another in love.[18]
11. Be kind and tenderhearted one to another.[19]
12. Forgive one another.[20]
13. Submit yourselves one to another.[21]
14. Comfort one another.[22]
15. Exhort one another.[23]
16. Consider one another.[24]
17. Provoke one another unto love and good works.[25]

18. Confess your faults one to another.[26]
19. Pray one for another.[27]
20. Have compassion one of another.[28]
21. Use hospitality one to another.[29]
22. Minister your gift one to another.[30]
23. Be subject one to another.[31]
24. Have fellowship one with another.[32]
25. Have the same care one for another.[33]

THE POWER OF EDIFYING ONE ANOTHER

In Acts 2:42, fellowship is listed after the apostles' doctrine. This is significant because the goal of fellowship is to produce spiritual maturity through mutual edification. One of the most effective ways to accomplish this is to provide opportunities for believers to give testimonies of God's working in their lives.

The incredible power of both prepared and spontaneous testimonies among believers is described to the Corinthian church by the Apostle Paul. "If therefore the whole church be come together into one place, and all speak with tongues, and there come in those that are unlearned, or unbelievers, will they not say that ye are mad?

"But if all prophesy, and there come in one that believeth not, or one unlearned, he is convinced of all, he is judged of all: And thus are the secrets of his heart made manifest; and so falling down on his face he will worship God, and report that God is in you of a truth."[34]

Notice the four things that will occur in the life of an unbeliever or an uninstructed believer if he encounters an assembly of those who are empowered by the Holy Spirit and are edifying one another:

1. The secrets of his heart will be exposed.
2. He will be convicted of his sins.
3. He will fall to his face and worship God.
4. He will acknowledge God is among you.

The word *prophesy* is explained in that same chapter. "But he that prophesieth speaketh unto men to edification, and exhortation, and comfort. He that speaketh in an unknown tongue edifieth himself; but he that prophesieth edifieth the church."[35]

The significance of having the fellowship of edification follow the teaching of the apostles' doctrine has a very important Biblical foundation and purpose. The essential content of the apostles' doctrine is the teaching of Jesus. He identified this teaching not as the *logos* of the Word but as the *rhema* of the Word.

"The words [*rhema*] that I speak unto you, they are spirit, and they are life."[36] "If ye abide in me, and my words [*rhema*] abide in you, ye shall ask what ye will, and it shall be done unto you."[37]

A *rhema* requires a confirmation of two or three witnesses. Thus, after the apostles' doctrine was presented, it was confirmed by the testimonies of those who were living it out. "In the mouth of two or three witnesses shall every word [*rhema*] be established."[38]

Based on this goal, Paul gives further instruction to the believers—whenever they meet together they should be ready to contribute a psalm, a piece of teaching, or a spiritual truth so that all might be edified.[39]

To "let everyone be ready" implies that the church leaders will meet personally with believers in order to give counsel, instruction, and training, so that when they meet together they will be ready to have something significant to share with the entire group.

This personal training between meetings was actually the method that Paul used in his work among believers. "As ye know how we exhorted and comforted and charged every one of you, as a father doth his children, That ye would walk worthy of God, who hath called you unto his kingdom and glory."[40] The general categories of testimonies are:

- A psalm (a message in sacred song)
- An instruction from Scripture
- A personal *rhema* from God's Word
- An insight into Christian living
- A report on how truth was applied

SPECIFIC TYPES OF EXHORTATIONS

The importance of believers exhorting each other on a regular basis is emphasized in the following passage. "Exhort one another daily, while it is called To-day; lest any of you be hardened through the deceitfulness of sin."[41]

The following types of exhortations should be shared by those who have prepared their hearts to seek the Lord, and who desire to glorify the Lord for what He is doing in their lives. "Let the redeemed of the LORD say so, whom he hath redeemed from the hand of the enemy."[42]

1. Building Faith by Sharing Rhemas

As each believer reads through the Scriptures, he or she should be looking for verses that stand out for personal application. These special verses are rhemas from God and build faith in those who receive them and in others who hear how they were worked out in daily living. "Faith cometh by hearing, and hearing by the word [*rhema*] of God."[43]

W. E. Vine's Expository Dictionary of New Testament Words explains the distinction between the *rhema* of the Word and the *logos* of the Word.

> The significance of *rhema* (as distinct from *logos*) is exemplified in the injunction to take "the sword of the Spirit, which is the word of God," Eph. 6:17; here the reference is not to the whole Bible as such, but to the individual scripture which the Spirit brings to our remembrance for use in time of need, a prerequisite being the regular storing of the mind with Scripture.[44]

2. Glorifying God by Answers to Prayer

The impossibilities of the Christian life are designed to motivate believers to cry out to the Lord and to seek His provision and protection through fervent prayer.

When God answers, the believer is responsible to glorify God by telling others what He did. "Call upon me in the day of trouble: I will deliver thee, and thou shalt glorify me."[45]

3. Encouraging Maturity by Biblical Disciplines

A disciple is a disciplined one. Jesus taught His disciples to carry out certain practices that would help them mature in the Christian life. He carried them out in His own life and promised special rewards to his disciples for doing them.

- Getting up early in the morning[46]
- Reading the Scriptures on a daily schedule[47]
- Turning Scripture into prayer[48]

- Quoting Scripture that was memorized[49]
- Fasting and praying for spiritual goals[50]
- Tithing and giving to the needs of others[51]
- Honoring the Lord's Day[52]

4. Describing How Salvation Took Place

There is nothing more thrilling than learning how the Lord worked in a person's life to bring him or her to salvation.

5. Explaining How Others Were Led to Christ

The obligation that believers have to share the Gospel with others is clearly stated in Scripture. "When I say unto the wicked, Thou shalt surely die; and thou givest him not warning, nor speakest to warn the wicked from his wicked way, to save his life; the same wicked man shall die in his iniquity; but his blood will I require at thine hand."[53]

As one believer gives a detailed report on how he led another person to Christ, others will benefit from this training in soul winning and be encouraged to do the same.

6. Explaining the Freedom of Biblical Principles

Just as there are physical laws that govern the universe, so there are spiritual laws that govern relationships with God and with others. These principles are opposite to our human nature. Therefore, they are most effectively presented by those who are personally applying them.

An effective way to present these principles is to give a four-part testimony based on these topics:

1. The problem I had in this area
2. Unsuccessful attempts to solve the problem

3. How I applied the Biblical principle

4. How God has worked in my life since then

The specific principles upon which these testimonies can be developed are explained in the Basic Seminar.[54]

- Acceptance of the way God made me[55]
- Obeying God-given authorities[56]
- Gaining a clear conscience[57]
- Forgiving those who have offended me[58]
- Yielding rights and rejoicing[59]
- Achieving moral purity[60]
- Discovering purpose through a life calling[61]

7. Tracing Illnesses to Spiritual Causes

Many diseases can be traced to a particular violation of a principle in God's Word, such as self-rejection, bitterness, guilt, anger, fear, worry, and anxiety.

When these spiritual causes are confessed and forsaken, the particular diseases they caused can be cleared up. We are hearing powerful testimonies from those who have experienced healing as a result of thorough self-examination and complete obedience to God's Word.

8. Sharing the Rewards of Suffering

God has promised to give the power of the Holy Spirit to those who successfully pass His tests, and it is important for believers to share about the types of sufferings God has allowed them to experience. They should then explain the deeper love, joy, peace, long-suffering, gentleness, goodness, faith, meekness, and temperance that resulted when they thanked God for the test and rejoiced in it.[62]

9. Passing on Wisdom From the Wise

God encourages us to walk with wise men so that we will be wise. Reading the biographies of great Christians is one way to gain wisdom. Then share the wisdom with others as you tell how their character and Godly standards were revealed and how they experienced victories through trials.

10. Reporting on the Results of Good Works

God created believers to be zealous of good works and to motivate each other to do good works. Most people need specific examples of things they could do to benefit others. Explaining good works in which you have participated and the results that came from them will be an inspiration to everyone.

11. Sharing the Benefits of Godly Standards

God challenges all believers to be "good soldiers" of Jesus Christ.[63] When a soldier voluntarily enlists in an army, he surrenders his individual freedom regarding the clothes he wears, the friends with whom he trains, the activities in which he engages, the music to which he marches, and the social life that he wants.

When the world sees uniformity and "quality control" of high standards among believers in these areas, they are attracted to the message. Reports of how high standards led to witnessing encourages others to adopt and maintain these standards.

12. Praising Others for Their Examples

One of the most powerful ways to edify is to give public praise of others for the character qualities they have demonstrated. Genuine praise involves pointing out a specific character quality that a person exhibited through his words, actions, or attitudes and then explaining how that action produced motivation in the observer to do the same.

THE POWERFUL POTENTIAL OF FELLOWSHIP

As various believers explain the work of the Lord in their lives, specific financial or material needs will certainly be made known. Simultaneously, the Holy Spirit will prompt other believers to meet these needs. Such generosity will provide further bonding within the fellowship.

The Greek word for *fellowship* is *koinonia*.[64] It means "partnership," to have interaction, and relates to distributing goods to those in need. From the word *common* comes the word *communion*,[65] which in Scripture is also translated from *koinonia*.

Paul describes this kind of fellowship as it took place among the Macedonian churches. "Moreover, brethren, we do you to wit of the grace of God bestowed on the churches of Macedonia; How that in a great trial of affliction the abundance of their joy and their deep poverty abounded unto the riches of their liberality.

"For to their power, I bear record, yea, and beyond their power they were willing of themselves; Praying us with much entreaty that we would receive the gift, and take upon us the fellowship [*koinonia*] of the ministering to the saints."[66]

THE REVIVALS FROM KOINONIA

Some of the greatest revivals in history were initiated and maintained by Spirit-led testimony meetings among those who had been trained in the teachings of Christ.

The great Welsh revivals at the beginning of the twentieth century were nonstop testimony meetings, that lasted for many weeks. Throngs of people waited outside for a chance to get into the packed church and take the place of those who were leaving. Those who were in the meeting would often be there as long as six to eight consecutive hours—unconscious of time—because of the powerful spirit of love and fellowship generated by the testimonies and interaction.

One man would give a tearful testimony of how Christ had brought him to repentance on a particular matter and how he had cleared his conscience. After this, a man or a woman with a beautiful voice would sing a confirming message in song. Then a recently converted drunkard would pray and, in his prayer, quote large passages of Scripture that he had memorized as a boy.

This, in turn, would prompt someone to call out, "I am not a believer, would someone show me how to get saved!" Everyone would bow in prayer as a mature Christian slipped over to that person and explained the way of salvation.

After the new believer repented and received Christ as Savior, he or she would stand and give a radiant testimony of how conversion had just taken place and explain the events that led up to it. The entire group would then break forth into joyful singing of a favorite song of praise for the salvation of this new believer.

These meetings went on twenty-four hours a day, seven days a week, week after week. They spread from city to city and ultimately impacted the world.[67]

Reaching the Lost by Feeding the Flock

Based on this and other examples, there is good reason for God's instruction to pastors to "feed the flock" and not just continually preach salvation messages. "So when they had dined, Jesus saith to Simon Peter, Simon, son of Jonas, lovest thou me more than these? He saith unto him, Yea, Lord; thou knowest that I love thee. He saith unto him, Feed my lambs.

"He saith to him again the second time, Simon, son of Jonas, lovest thou me? He saith unto him, Yea, Lord; thou knowest that I love thee. He saith unto him, Feed my sheep.

"He saith unto him the third time, Simon, son of Jonas, lovest thou me? Peter was grieved because he said unto him the third time, Lovest thou me? And he said unto him, Lord, thou knowest all things; thou knowest that I love thee. Jesus saith unto him, Feed my sheep."[68]

Peter's comprehension of this command is reflected in his instruction to bishops. "Feed the flock of God which is among you, taking the oversight thereof, not by constraint, but willingly; not for filthy lucre, but of a ready mind."[69]

Someone has wisely observed, "The shepherd should feed the sheep, because shepherds do not reproduce sheep; sheep reproduce sheep."[70]

The Dynamic of First-Century Testimonies

The first-century Church did not survive *in spite of* persecution—it thrived *because of* persecution.

All the believers were taught by the apostles' doctrine that whenever they experienced trials or persecutions they would have a corresponding measure of glory and the Spirit of God upon them.

This, in turn, would increase their ability to love God and others.

The Apostle Paul confirmed this truth to the Corinthian church. "And he said unto me, My grace is sufficient for thee: for my strength is made perfect in weakness. Most gladly therefore will I rather glory in my infirmities, that the power of Christ may rest upon me. Therefore I take pleasure in infirmities, in reproaches, in necessities, in persecutions, in distresses for Christ's sake: for when I am weak, then am I strong."[71]

The apostles not only taught this principle, they also demonstrated it in their own lives. When they were arrested, thrown into prison, and beaten for proclaiming the teachings of Jesus, they rejoiced "that they were counted worthy to suffer shame for his name."[72]

What an amazing outlook! Yet it is completely consistent with the teachings of Jesus to rejoice and be exceeding glad when such persecutions come, because our reward in Heaven will be great.

The Basis of Sacrificial Generosity

The testimonies in these first-century assemblies undoubtedly included vibrant reports of those who had suffered for their faith and experienced more of the power of Christ. Those who suffered financial loss would not lack, because others would be prompted by the Holy Spirit to give to their needs, thus "distributing to the necessity of saints."[73]

There was such rejoicing over suffering that Paul added an important warning to be certain that it was not a result of their own wrongdoing. "But let none of you suffer as a murderer, or as a thief, or as an evildoer, or as a busybody in other men's matters."[74]

WHY REVIVALS DO NOT "JUST HAPPEN"

After years of amazing revival experience, Charles Finney made the observation that if farmers would plan for crops the way the Church plans for revivals, we all would have starved long ago.[75]

Just as there are laws of the harvest, so there are spiritual laws that must be followed to experience and maintain revivals. We reap what we sow, we reap where we sow, we reap more than we sow, and we reap in a different season than we sow.

In my early years of youth work, I had the privilege of being the youth director for several different churches. I was committed to memorizing and meditating on the teachings of Scripture, especially the Sermon on the Mount. As I experienced the rewards Jesus promised for such disciplines as prayer, fasting, giving, and clearing my conscience with those whom I had offended, I enthusiastically explained these disciplines to the young people and challenged them to do the same.

The results were both thrilling and predictable as young people gave testimonies of how they had applied the truths of God's Word and experienced the joy and freedom that result from obedience. During the week, I would personally meet with teenagers and help them take one step forward in these disciplines. As they experienced results, I would ask them to give a testimony to the youth group the following Sunday evening.

In one youth group in Chicago's Northshore area, we enjoyed spontaneous testimonies every Sunday evening for about two years. The group began with twenty and grew to over two hundred.[76]

With this experience, I served other youth groups for a six-month period. We would begin with a weekend conference explaining the principles of

Christ's teachings and the rewards that He gives to those who follow His disciplines. Then, after six months of personal counseling, we had another retreat. During this time, I could count on a revival breaking out through the testimonies of the young people. The transformations in lives were genuine and lasting.[77]

On another occasion, I met with three hundred young men for a weeklong conference. About twenty in the group were very rebellious and had bonded together in resistance to the teaching.

During the week, I talked to several of these young men individually. This gave me opportunity to discover their greatest points of resistance and help them make important decisions to clear their lives in these areas. I then asked each one if he would give a public testimony of his commitment. All agreed to do so.

After about four days, we began an evening session by asking all those who had allowed Christ to work in their lives to come forward and give a testimony. As some of these rebellious fellows walked forward, their friends were stunned and listened carefully to what they had to say.

Soon others came forward to confess things that were wrong in their lives and to ask forgiveness. Then more rebels went out and called their parents to confess things they had done and to ask forgiveness.

When they returned to the meeting, their faces shone. They would then give a testimony to the whole group. This revival continued until about one or two o'clock in the morning. The young men that were turned around in that revival are some of the strongest leaders we have today in the Institute in Basic Life Principles ministry.[78]

The Predictability of Revivals

One day, I was asked by the leader of a missionary organization to speak to several hundred sons and daughters of missionaries at their missions school in Bolivia. He explained that many of the young people were extremely bitter and rebellious. Since I would be there only ten days, I decided to follow the same pattern of explaining the teachings of Jesus to the whole group and then have personal conferences to help individuals apply them in their lives. On the fifth day, the leader opened the evening session with a song. Suddenly, a young man stood up and asked the whole group to forgive him for his wrong attitudes in the school.

When he finished, another young man stood up and said he had been bitter toward his teachers and had asked them to forgive him. When a third fellow stood up, the leader sat down and the testimonies continued throughout the evening. They were interspersed with appropriate songs and specific prayers.

At one o'clock in the morning, the school officials asked if we should let it continue or stop it. I pointed out that there were still a few student leaders that had not yet made things right with the Lord and with others. Soon these also responded to the conviction of the Holy Spirit and repented before the Lord.[79]

About twenty years later, those who had been in that meeting wanted to get together for a reunion. About one hundred met for that special event, and many recalled how the revival that night was the turning point in their lives.[80]

A few years ago, a school superintendent in Ohio anguished over the carnality and lack of spiritual interest among his students, especially the high school students. I offered to come to his school and present the same ministry that had been so effective in bringing revivals in the past. The teaching sessions began Monday.

By Wednesday, the Spirit of God prompted students, teachers, and parents to publicly confess bitterness and wrongdoing and ask individuals in the group to forgive them. The spontaneous testimonies continued the next day when the students returned to school, and many spiritual victories were won.[81]

How Testimonies Overcome Satan

Scripture instructs believers to give public testimony of God's work in their lives.[82] The power of such testimonies is further confirmed in the following Scripture: "And they overcame him [the accuser of our brethren—Satan] by the blood of the Lamb, and by the word of their testimony; and they loved not their lives unto the death."[83] Notice that conquering the fear of death is related to testimonies that overcome Satan.

The most powerful people on the face of the earth are those who have no fear of death. Jesus died to deliver us from this fear. "That through death he might destroy him that had the power of death, that is, the devil; And deliver them who through fear of death were all their lifetime subject to bondage."[84]

In order for a person to give a testimony, he must overcome the fear of man and die to his own pride. This death to self produces an immediate spirit of glory and of God on the person who is giving the testimony, and the love that results impacts the lives of all those around him.

The Biblical Basis of Clarifying the Word

In a very real sense, testimonies are living commentaries on Scriptures that have been applied to daily living. In the days of Ezra and Nehemiah, the Law was read to all the people, but only after the priests caused them to understand the sense of it did revival break out.

"So they read in the book in the law of God distinctly, and gave the sense, and caused them to understand the reading. . . . For all the people wept, when they heard the words of the law."[85]

Nehemiah wisely redirected their mourning to a seven-day gathering during which they sought the face of the Lord and enjoyed fellowship with each other.

At the end of this time, a deeper revival took place. "And they stood up in their place, and read in the book of the law of the LORD their God one fourth part of the day; and another fourth part they confessed, and worshipped the LORD their God."[86]

Testimonies are effective because every person has similar experiences. "There hath no temptation taken you but such as is common to man: but God is faithful, who will not suffer you to be tempted above that ye are able; but will with the temptation also make a way to escape, that ye may be able to bear it."[87]

Motivating One Another to Share

During a revival many testimonies will be spontaneous. However, the leader should not assume this will take place; he should know before the meeting begins who is prepared to give a testimony. He should also encourage them to be the first ones to give their testimonies.

When D. L. Moody began attending a church in Chicago, the leader would ask for testimonies, but no one would get up and give one. The silence was deadening to the spirit of the meeting. Dwight Moody decided to do something about the problem.

He approached one of the deacons and said, "Would you be willing to prepare a testimony and be ready to give it at the next meeting?" The deacon agreed to do this. Then Dwight asked him if he would lead off the testimony time. To this the man agreed.

He then went to two more men in the church with the same request. He asked each one to be the first to stand up to give a testimony. Each one agreed, without knowing that the other men were also planning to be the first to stand up to share a testimony.

When the time came time for the testimony meeting, the pastor gave his usual request, "Does anyone have a testimony for the Lord?" He did not know what Dwight Moody had done, and suddenly three men stood up to give a testimony.

The pastor was surprised, and the entire group was encouraged. Others also stood and gave testimonies as a spirit of revival broke out in the meeting.[88]

Sometimes a person will share something that is Scripturally inaccurate or inappropriate. The leader must be ready to graciously correct him when it is necessary or, if more appropriate, contact the individual after the meeting to clarify his understanding of the truth.

Notes

1. Acts 5:13.
2. I John 2:19.
3. I John 2:20.
4. James Strong, S.T.D., LL.D, *Strong's Exhaustive Concordance of the Bible,* McDonald Publishing Company, McClean, Virginia, *#5545.*
5. I Corinthians 5:13.
6. II Corinthians 2:7.
7. Ephesians 4:11–12.
8. Hebrews 10:24–25.
9. I Peter 1:22.
10. Romans 12:10.
11. Ibid.
12. Romans 12:16.
13. Romans 14:19.
14. Romans 15:7.
15. Romans 15:14.
16. II Corinthians 13:12.
17. Galatians 5:13.
18. Ephesians 4:2.
19. Ephesians 4:32.
20. Ibid.
21. Ephesians 5:21.
22. I Thessalonians 4:18.
23. Hebrews 3:13.
24. Hebrews 10:24.
25. Ibid.
26. James 5:16.
27. Ibid.
28. I Peter 3:8.
29. I Peter 4:9.
30. I Peter 4:10.
31. I Peter 5:5.
32. I John 1:7.
33. I Corinthians 12:25.
34. I Corinthians 14:23–25.
35. I Corinthians 14:3–4.
36. John 6:63.
37. John 15:7.
38. II Corinthians 13:1.
39. I Corinthians 14:26.
40. I Thessalonians 2:11–12.
41. Hebrews 3:13.
42. Psalm 107:2.
43. Romans 10:17.
44. W. E. Vine, Merrill F. Unger, William White, Jr., *Vine's Complete Expository Dictionary of Old and New Testament Words,* Thomas Nelson Publishers, Nashville, 1996, p. 683.
45. Psalm 50:15.
46. Mark 1:35.
47. I Peter 2:2.
48. John 15:7.
49. Psalm 1:2–3, Luke 4:3–14.
50. Matthew 6:16–18.
51. Matthew 6:4.
52. Isaiah 58:13–14.
53. Ezekiel 3:18.
54. Institute in Basic Life Principles, Basic Life Principles Seminar. For information, call 630-323-9800.
55. Psalm 139:14.
56. Romans 13:1.
57. I Timothy 1:19.
58. Matthew 6:14–15.
59. Philippians 2:5-8.
60. Galatians 5:16–17.
61. Jeremiah 29:11.
62. Galatians 5:22–23.
63. II Timothy 2:3.
64. James Strong, S.T.D., LL.D, *Strong's Exhaustive Concordance of the Bible,* McDonald Publishing Company, McClean, Virginia, *#2842.*
65. *Webster's Third New International Dictionary,* Merriam-Webster, Inc., Springfield, Massachusetts, 1981, p. 460.
66. II Corinthians 8:1–4.
67. David Matthews, *I Saw the Welsh Revival,* Moody Press, Chicago, 1951, pp. 59–69.
68. John 21:15–17.
69. I Peter 5:2.
70. Author Unknown.
71. II Corinthians 12:9–10.
72. Acts 5:41.
73. Romans 12:13.
74. I Peter 4:15.
75. Charles G. Finney, "Revival Lecture I, 'What a Revival of Religion Is,'" *Revivals of Religion,* Fleming H. Revell Company, Westwood, New Jersey, pp. 5–6.
76. Winnetka Bible Church.
77. First Baptist Church, Elmhurst.
78. Young Men's Counseling Seminar, Northwoods Conference Center.
79. New Tribes Mission, Tambo School in Bolivia.
80. IBLP Headquarters, Oak Brook, Illinois.
81. Mansfield Christian School, Mansfield, Ohio.
82. Psalm 107:2.
83. Revelation 12:11.
84. Hebrews 2:14–15.
85. Nehemiah 8:8–9.
86. Nehemiah 9:3.
87. I Corinthians 10:13.
88. This story is told of D. L. Moody and his early contacts with the Chicago church.

Confession is discreetly telling others about our secret faults so that God does not get blamed for the consequences.

"He that covereth his sins shall not prosper: but whoso confesseth and forsaketh them shall have mercy."

—*Proverbs 28:13*

Chapter 5

THE POWER OF ITS COMMUNION

Chapter Summary

*P*urity of doctrine and richness of fellowship are so vital for the health and outreach of the local church that there must be continual self-examination in order for these to be maintained. This is the purpose of observing communion, which must include a systematic and thorough procedure for self-examination. The goal of communion is to renew the blood covenant with Christ and enable the Body of Christ to discern how to perfect itself in love. Communion is to the Church what the liver is to the body. If impurities are not removed, the body will become weak and sickly and die prematurely. Those who partake of communion without thorough self-examination will experience the same consequences.

The apostles' doctrine and fellowship were so vital to the health and growth of the first-century Church that God established the Lord's Table to ensure that nothing diminished the purity or power of the Church's members.

Communion is in itself a powerful aspect of the Church. It is so powerful, in fact, that if believers do not properly carry it out, they will experience physical weakness, sickness, or even premature death.

"But let a man examine himself, and so let him eat of that bread, and drink of that cup. For he that eateth and drinketh unworthily, eateth and drinketh damnation to himself, not discerning the Lord's body. For this cause many are weak and sickly among you, and many sleep."[1]

WHAT IS "DISCERNING THE LORD'S BODY"?

Discerning the Lord's body is very important, because failure to do so is the stated cause of many believers becoming weak and sick and dying prematurely.[2]

The body of Christ has a twofold meaning. It refers to His physical body, which was given for our redemption.[3] However, the body of Christ also refers to His spiritual body, which is made up of all true believers.

This "mystery" of the body of Christ is explained by Paul. "For we are members of his body, of his flesh, and of his bones."[4] As such, we are also members with every other believer. "Now ye are the body of Christ, and members in particular.[5]

Since every believer is joined together in one Body, whatever one believer does to another, he does to himself. If he refuses to forgive an offending brother, he is actually refusing to forgive himself and refusing to experience God's forgiveness. This clarifies the doctrine of Christ: "But if ye forgive not men their trespasses, neither will your Father forgive your trespasses."[6]

If one believer rejects another believer, he is actually rejecting himself. This truth is explained by Paul in the following discourse:

"For as the body is one, and hath many members, and all the members of that one body, being many, are one body: so also is Christ. . . . But now are they many members, yet but one body. And the eye cannot say unto the hand, I have no need of thee: nor again the head to the feet, I have no need of you. Nay, much more those members of the body, which seem to be more feeble, are necessary."[7]

THE CORPORATE SIN OF ONE MEMBER

Every believer is a member of the Body of Christ, and therefore, one believer's sin causes the whole Body to sin. This is an awesome truth. It is also taught in the Old Testament. When Achan committed his secret sin, he was a member of the nation of Israel, and God judged the entire nation for sinning.

"But the children of Israel committed a trespass in the accursed thing: for Achan, the son of Carmi, the son of Zabdi, the son of Zerah, of the tribe of Judah, took of the accursed thing: and the anger of the LORD was kindled against the children of Israel."[8]

This corporate consequence of sin is affirmed by Paul. "Know ye not that your bodies [plural] are the members of Christ? shall I [singular] then take the members [plural] of Christ, and make them the members of an harlot? God forbid."[9]

Thus when one member sins, he offends the entire body and will be judged for the deeds that he has done in his body. "For we must all appear before the judgment seat of Christ; that every one may receive the things done in his body, according to that he hath done, whether it be good or bad."[10]

Jesus referred to His body as the Temple,[11] and in the New Testament, we learn that our bodies are the temple of the Holy Spirit. To sin against the temple is to bring God's judgment. "What? know ye not that your body is the temple of the Holy Ghost which is in you, which ye have of God, and ye are not your own?"[12] "If any man defile the temple of God, him shall God destroy; for the temple of God is holy, which temple ye are."[13]

How Does Unworthiness Produce Disease?

God's warning on the misuse of communion is serious. "Wherefore whosoever shall eat this bread, and drink this cup of the Lord, unworthily, shall be guilty of the body and blood of the Lord. But let a man examine himself, and so let him eat of that bread, and drink of that cup. For he that eateth and drinketh unworthily, eateth and drinketh damnation to himself, not discerning the Lord's body. For this cause many are weak and sickly among you, and many sleep. For if we would judge ourselves, we should not be judged. But when we are judged, we are chastened of the Lord, that we should not be condemned with the world."[14]

One of the tragedies in modern America is that in spite of the billions of dollars that are spent on medical care, the people of our nation are becoming more and more unhealthy. It is estimated that about 50 percent of Americans are afflicted with a chronic illness. This means that they have a medical condition that will require medication the rest of their lives. What is even more tragic is that there are as many sick people in the church as there are out of the church, and in many cases, prayer for the sick seems to have little effect.

The problem is that sick people are looking to doctors or diets for a cure, rather than going to the spiritual source of the problem and resolving that first. A doctor or a diet may treat the symptoms of osteoporosis, which is a softening of the bones. However, in order to be cured of the disease, a person must deal with its causes, two of which Scripture identifies as envy and jealousy. "A sound heart is the life of the flesh: but envy the rottenness of the bones."[15]

Medications can be given to treat heart disease. However, both the Scripture and medical textbooks identify fear and anxiety as a primary cause of angina, coronary artery disease, and heart attacks. Jesus made clear this relationship when He said, "Men's hearts failing them for fear."[16]

In many cases, individuals experience healing of diseases and infirmities when spiritual root causes can be identified and dealt with Scripturally.

In his ministry, Jesus combined healing with preaching, and He sent His disciples to do the same. When church members become sick, they should first call for the elders. It is the elders' responsibility to determine whether or not that person has a sickness because of sin against the Body of Christ. If so, there must be confession of sin before healing takes place.[17]

How to Have Effective Communion Services

In order to avoid ineffective or improper communion services, church leaders would be wise to develop a systematic way to lead the church members through effective personal examination before communion is taken. One possible approach would be to each week select a character quality that Christ taught and then create a series of probing questions to determine if that quality is being consistently carried out in the life of each believer.

If there has been a failure to demonstrate the quality, and others have been offended or damaged, the instruction of Jesus should be followed: "Leave there thy gift before the altar, and go thy way; first be reconciled to thy brother, and then come and offer thy gift."[18]

An Example of a Character Examination

The following presentation is an example of leading a study on the Biblical perspectives of a particular character quality and helping all the believers examine their own lives in the light of that quality.

This week, let us examine our consistency in demonstrating the quality of punctuality. Punctuality is based on two important factors. The first is a reverence for time, and the second is a respect for other people.

We reverence time because God created it. He created days, nights, weeks, months, and years. He also established seasons of the year and seasons of one's lifetime. God designed the day for work and the night for rest. He wants us to make full use of every day and finish a week's work in six days.

We are then to honor Him with the "firstfruits" of all our increase, including the first portion of our paycheck, the first part of the day, and the first day of the week.

"Have you been punctual:
- *In your morning appointments with God?*
- *In getting to bed early, so you can rise early?*
- *In being at church services on time?*
- *In giving your offerings to the Lord?*
- *In praying for a need you learn about?*

- *In giving to others' needs as God directs?*
- *In witnessing to those who need salvation?*

If we have not been punctual toward God, consider the Word of the Lord, "Therefore to him that knoweth to do good, and doeth it not, to him it is sin."[19] Confess your sins to God and write out the steps you are going to take to establish punctuality before the Lord.

The second factor required for punctuality is a respect for other people and the time God has entrusted to them. Time is one of our most precious assets. We are given a limited amount of it, and each of us must provide an account to God of how we use it.

When we keep other people waiting, we rob them of their time and hinder them in being punctual. We fail to obey the command to "walk circumspectly . . . Redeeming the time, because the days are evil."[20] We also fail to comprehend the truth in the following poem:

"Lost yesterday,
somewhere between sunrise and sunset,
two golden hours,
each set with sixty diamond minutes.
They will never be found;
they are lost forever."[21]

Are you punctual:

- *For mealtimes and other family gatherings?*
- *For work at your place of employment?*
- *For appointments you make with others?*
- *In paying bills that you owe?*
- *In writing thank-you letters and notes?*
- *In returning books?*

If we have robbed others of time by our lack of punctuality, let us now make a list of those whom we have wronged and ask forgiveness. Let us be prompt to fulfill our commitments and ask others to hold us accountable for punctuality. Make this a priority until punctuality is a consistent discipline in your life.

Another approach to thorough self-examination is to focus on one of the Ten Commandments each week. After explaining its full implication, ask a series of questions that will indicate whether the commandment has been obeyed or violated.

THE DEEPER SIGNIFICANCE OF COMMUNION

When Jesus established communion with His disciples in the upper room,[22] He presented it as a blood covenant. His disciples were very familiar with the symbolism and meaning of this sacred procedure, which God carried out with Abraham.[23] Such a covenant contains lifelong commitments and obligations for those who enter into it.

By studying the rich meaning of the blood covenant, and presenting it to the congregation, the communion service will take on a whole new significance and seriousness.

THE POWER OF COMMUNION IN SMALL CHURCHES

Small churches have a powerful potential to impact their communities with the love and truth of the Gospel. However, because the members and families are often so closely associated, it is easy for innocent words or actions to be misunderstood and cause deep damage in the fellowship. "A whisperer separateth chief friends,"[24] and "the words of a talebearer are as wounds, and they go down into the innermost parts of the belly."[25]

Because of this danger, it is vitally important for smaller churches to have more frequent times of communion so that any hurt feelings can be cleared up quickly.

On this point, it is important to distinguish between a "home church," which involves one family whose members worship together, and churches that meet in homes, where several families come together. Scripture is clear on the need for a fellowship larger than one family because God has ordained two distinct jurisdictions—one for the family and one for the church. A "one-family church" violates this distinction.

"Not forsaking the assembling of ourselves together, as the manner of some is; but exhorting one another: and so much the more, as ye see the day approaching."[26]

In our day, as in the first century, many churches begin in a home and then outgrow the home. Following are some references to such churches in the first century.

"And daily in the temple, and in every house, they ceased not to teach and preach Jesus Christ."[27]

"Likewise greet the church that is in their house. Salute my well-beloved Epaenetus, who is the firstfruits of Achaia unto Christ."[28]

"The churches of Asia salute you. Aquila and Priscilla salute you much in the Lord, with the church that is in their house."[29]

"Salute the brethren which are in Laodicea, and Nymphas, and the church which is in his house."[30]

In recent years, there has been a phenomenal growth in the Christian community in mainland China. When one of the leading pastors was asked about the reason for their growth, he said, "Before 1949, we practiced Christianity in churches, and hardly anywhere else. After the persecutions, we practiced it in our homes, and therefore everywhere else!"[31]

The dynamic of this movement is further explained. "The strength of the Chinese revival resulted from the outward form of the church being smashed. Believers continued in homes and churches organized around family lines and neighborhoods.

"It was not the institutional church that primarily revived in China, but the house churches. Perhaps the secret was that Christianity became 'rubbed in' to Chinese culture, embedding itself in families, sitting rooms and apartment blocks in a way it never had before."[32]

The Requirement of a Clear Conscience

One of the primary purposes for communion is to establish a clear conscience with God and others. A good conscience is so vital that the Apostle Paul named it, along with faith, as the chief weapon to protect believers from spiritual disaster. "Holding faith, and a good conscience; which some having put away concerning faith have made shipwreck."[33]

Paul's constant goal was to maintain a good conscience before God and others. "And herein do I exercise myself, to have always a conscience void of offence toward God, and toward men."[34]

Because sickness is one of the consequences of neglecting or violating communion, believers were to call the elders of the church when they were sick and confess any sins or faults that had not been dealt with.

"Is any sick among you? let him call for the elders of the church; and let them pray over him, anointing him with oil in the name of the Lord: And the prayer of faith shall save the sick, and the Lord shall raise him up; and if he have committed sins, they shall be forgiven him. Confess your faults one to another, and pray one for another, that ye may be healed. The effectual fervent prayer of a righteous man availeth much."[35]

Notice that clearing up offenses with God and with others is an essential preparation for effectual, fervent prayer. This gives further significance to the sequence of Acts 2:42. They met together for first, the apostles' doctrine, then fellowship, then communion, and finally prayer. If a group of believers expects to have powerful times of prayer, they must first have effective times of communion.

God warns that if a husband and wife are not in total fellowship, their prayers will be hindered. "Likewise, ye husbands, dwell with them according to knowledge, giving honour unto the wife, as unto the weaker vessel, and as being heirs together of the grace of life; that your prayers be not hindered."[36]

God also warns that if a believer allows sin to continue in his life, God will not hear his prayers. "If I regard iniquity in my heart, the Lord will not hear me."[37] "He that covereth his sins shall not prosper: but whoso confesseth and forsaketh them shall have mercy."[38]

HOW OFTEN SHOULD COMMUNION BE OBSERVED?

The first-century Church observed communion on a far more frequent and regular basis than we do today. It was one of the four vital functions in which all the disciples continued steadfastly.

In our day, few local churches observe the Lord's Table once a week. Many do it once a month, and some do it once a quarter or once a year. It is little wonder that there are so many factions, divisions, and church splits. Even those who observe the Lord's Table more regularly need to guard against the tendency to view it as a mundane ritual.

Notes

1. I Corinthians 11:28–30.
2. I Corinthians 11:29–30.
3. Revelation 5:9.
4. Ephesians 5:30.
5. I Corinthians 12:27.
6. Matthew 6:15.
7. I Corinthians 12:12, 20–22.
8. Joshua 7:1.
9. I Corinthians 6:15.
10. II Corinthians 5:10.
11. John 2:21.
12. I Corinthians 6:19.
13. I Corinthians 3:17.
14. I Corinthians 11:27–32.
15. Proverbs 14:30.
16. Luke 21:26.
17. James 5:14–16.
18. Matthew 5:24.
19. James 4:17.
20. Ephesians 5:15–16.
21. Poem Mr. Gothard learned as a student at Ogden Avenue School.
22. I Corinthians 11:23.
23. Genesis 15:7–18.
24. Proverbs 16:28.
25. Proverbs 18:8.
26. Hebrews 10:25.
27. Acts 5:42.
28. Romans 16:5.
29. I Corinthians 16:19.
30. Colossians 4:15.
31. Alex Buchan, *Open Doors Newsbrief*, Volume 15, Number 1, January 2000.
32. Ibid.
33. I Timothy 1:19.
34. Acts 24:16.
35. James 5:14–16.
36. I Peter 3:7.
37. Psalm 66:18.
38. Proverbs 28:13.

Prayer is the discipline of transforming our mind to think God's thoughts and then talking to the King in the King's own language.

———————————

"For my thoughts are not your
thoughts, neither are your ways
my ways, saith the LORD.
For as the heavens are higher than the
earth, so are my ways higher than
your ways, and my thoughts than
your thoughts."

—Isaiah 55:8–9

Chapter

6

THE POWER OF ITS PRAYER

Chapter Summary

℘rayer in the first-century Church was not just ordinary prayer. It had unusual power that caused entire cities to realize that the believers were worshiping a living God Who was all-powerful and all-knowing. The difference between their fervent, effectual prayer and average prayer is the same as the difference between a laser beam and diffused light. The laser beam and powerful prayer both occur when there is total uniformity among the elements. Specific types of prayer, positions in prayer, wrestling with principalities, and crying out to God all add vital dimensions to effective prayer.

The apostles' doctrine, fellowship, and communion were critical to carrying out the fourth and most important function of the first-century Church—fervent, effectual prayer.

When the disciples were in one accord with God and each other, there was power in their prayers. "And when they had prayed, the place was shaken where they were assembled together;

and they were all filled with the Holy Ghost, and they spake the word of God with boldness."[1]

What Name Describes God's Church?

There are several names that are used to identify New Testament churches, such as the church of God,[2] the church of the living God,[3] church of the Firstborn,[4] and the names of cities in which the churches were located.[5]

Jesus referred to the Temple as a house of prayer. Every believer is a temple of the Holy Spirit. However, as they meet together, it can also be said that they become a house of prayer. "It is written, My house shall be called the house of prayer."[6] The universal application of this name is indicated by the account in the Book of Mark. "Is it not written, My house shall be called of all nations the house of prayer?"[7]

The Old Testament reference of this name is Isaiah 56:7. "Even them will I bring to my holy mountain, and make them joyful in my house of prayer . . . for mine house shall be called an house of prayer for all people."

People everywhere are as open to sincere prayer for their special needs as they are for the genuine love that ought to motivate prayer. Prayer leaps over barriers and breaks down walls.

How Prayer Unites the Body of Christ

The Body of Christ consists of thousands of smaller units throughout the world. Each one is like a separate cell, and they can all be united through the means of prayer. Prayer is like the nervous system, which alerts the body when an injury has taken place. In the physical body and in the Body of Christ, when one member suffers, all the members suffer with it.[8]

We are commanded to "do good unto all men, especially unto them who are of the household of faith."[9] The household of faith is much bigger than one church. It includes true believers from all churches.

One way to do good to fellow believers is to pray for them. This is precisely the instruction we are given in Scripture: "Praying always with all prayer and supplication in the Spirit, and watching thereunto with all perseverance and supplication for all saints."[10]

Our prayers for other believers ought to be similar to one of the prayers given by Paul. Notice how this prayer emphasizes the love and power that will cause the Church to triumph.

"For this cause I bow my knees unto the Father of our Lord Jesus Christ, Of whom the whole family in heaven and earth is named, That he would grant you, according to the riches of his glory, to be strengthened with might by his Spirit in the inner man;

"That Christ may dwell in your hearts by faith; that ye, being rooted and grounded in love, May be able to comprehend with all saints what is the breadth, and length, and depth, and height; And to know the love of Christ, which passeth knowledge, that ye might be filled with all the fulness of God.

"Now unto him that is able to do exceeding abundantly above all that we ask or think, according to the power that worketh in us, Unto him be glory in the church by Christ Jesus throughout all ages, world without end. Amen."[11]

Paul's first instruction to Timothy was not to give better sermons or create more church activities, but to pray and teach the believers how to pray.

"I exhort therefore, that, first of all, supplications, prayers, intercessions, and giving of thanks, be made for all men."[12] This instruction then identifies a significant group of people for whom we are to pray—"for kings, and for all that are in authority."

The results of praying effectively for leaders are phenomenal—"that we may lead a quiet and peaceable life in all godliness and honesty. For this is good and acceptable in the sight of God our Saviour; Who will have all men to be saved, and to come unto the knowledge of the truth."[13]

In this passage, we have both a command and a strategy to effectively reach the world with the Gospel of Jesus Christ—through fervent, effectual prayers for all leaders and all those under their jurisdictions. "All that are in authority" would include these:

1. All government officials
2. All presidents of companies
3. All pastors of local churches
4. All community leaders and family leaders

An effective way to pray for these leaders is to make opportunities to meet them and get acquainted with them and their specific needs for prayer. Anyone who does this on a consistent basis will discover that leaders usually have one or more of the following major concerns:

1. Marriage conflicts
2. Rebellious sons or daughters

3. Financial problems

4. Physical ailments

As you talk with the leaders of your community, they will usually have a boldness and openness in telling you about their problems. They will be open to solutions if you have some proven information that you can give to help them solve their problems, and they will usually be very appreciative of prayer on their behalf.

God will often show His supernatural power by answering a prayer for a leader in such a way that the leader knows it could have been only the Lord who did it. When God answers such prayer, that leader will often want those under his authority to discover the very things he experienced.

WHAT ARE THE TYPES OF PRAYER?

Paul describes four types of prayer. They are supplications, prayers, intercessions, and giving of thanks.[14]

1. What is supplication?

Supplication is a penitent appeal for God's mercy. We have all turned from God and His ways and deserve His judgment. The ultimate judgment of God upon a nation is the scattering of its families.[15]

This is what is now happening around the world as sons and daughters are being separated from their parents and led into the bondage of addictions, rebellion, gangs, and immorality. Parents are divorcing each other, and grandparents are being estranged from their grandchildren.

God promises, "If my people, which are called by my name, shall humble themselves, and pray, and seek my face, and turn from their wicked ways; then will I hear from heaven, and will forgive their sin, and will heal their land."[16]

Daniel records a powerful prayer of supplication: "Now therefore, O our God, hear the prayer of thy servant, and his supplications, and cause thy face to shine upon thy sanctuary that is desolate, for the Lord's sake.

"O my God, incline thine ear, and hear; open thine eyes, and behold our desolations, and the city which is called by thy name: for we do not present our supplications before thee for our righteousnesses, but for thy great mercies.

"O Lord, hear; O Lord, forgive; O Lord, hearken and do; defer not, for thine own sake, O my God: for thy city and thy people are called by thy name."[17]

2. What is prayer?

After an initial time of supplication, we are to offer various prayers for those in authority. Prayer is not asking God to fulfill our selfish desires; it is asking God to fulfill His Word and His will.[18]

When we have a particular "burden" or concern for a person or situation, it may be an indication that God is waiting to fulfill a specific prayer in that area. An example of this is Nehemiah's concern for the condition of the remnant in Jerusalem, his subsequent prayer and fasting over the matter, and God's provision and direction through the king.[19]

One of the most effective ways to pray is to explain to God how His enemies are coming not against us but against Him and His work.

A good example of this is Hezekiah's prayer. "O LORD God of Israel, which dwellest between the cherubims, thou art the God, even thou alone, of all the kingdoms of the earth; thou hast made heaven and earth.

"LORD, bow down thine ear, and hear: open, LORD, thine eyes, and see: and hear the words of Sennacherib, which hath sent him to reproach the living God. Of a truth, LORD, the kings of Assyria have destroyed the nations and their lands, And have cast their gods into the fire: for they were no gods, but the work of men's hands, wood and stone: therefore they have destroyed them.

"Now therefore, O LORD our God, I beseech thee, save thou us out of his hand, that all the kingdoms of the earth may know that thou art the LORD God, even thou only."[20]

In one sense, prayer is simply allowing the Holy Spirit to communicate God's thoughts back to Him through our words. This is initially done by turning Scripture into prayer. God has exalted His Word and loves to hear us use it when praying to Him. "And he that searcheth the hearts knoweth what is the mind of the Spirit, because he maketh intercession for the saints according to the will of God."[21]

When we ask for something according to God's will, He immediately gives it to us. However, it is then our responsibility to seek and find that which He has given and "knock on doors" to bring it to pass.

Many believers think God did not hear their prayers, because they did not see immediate results after asking for something. However, Jesus assures us that everyone who asks receives. "For every one that asketh receiveth; and he that seeketh findeth; and to him that knocketh it shall be opened."[22]

Prayer involves engaging in spiritual warfare against Satan, because "we wrestle not against flesh and blood, but against principalities, against powers, against the rulers of the darkness of this world, against spiritual wickedness in high places."[23]

When two believers agree in faith about a need, the power of Satan is restrained in that area. "Again I say unto you, That if two of you shall agree on earth as touching any thing that they shall ask, it shall be done for them of my Father which is in heaven."[24]

For major needs, fasting should be combined with prayer; this increases spiritual alertness. Christ promised that if we fast secretly, He would reward us openly.[25] One reward is that our judgment will be as clear and bright as the noon day.[26]

Prayer is an attitude of total, continuous dependence upon God.[27] With this attitude, we are able to fulfill the instruction to pray without ceasing.[28] God encourages us to be persistent in prayer when dealing with oppressive situations. To illustrate this, He gives the example of the widow and the unjust judge.

"There was in a city a judge, which feared not God, neither regarded man: And there was a widow in that city; and she came unto him, saying, Avenge me of mine adversary. And he would not for a while: but afterward he said within himself, Though I fear not God, nor regard man;

"Yet because this widow troubleth me, I will avenge her, lest by her continual coming she weary me. And the Lord said, Hear what the unjust judge saith. And shall not God avenge his own elect, which cry day and night unto him, though he bear long with them? I tell you that he will avenge them speedily. Nevertheless when the Son of man cometh, shall he find faith on the earth?"[29]

It is important to record and report to others God's answers to prayer, so He can be glorified. "Call upon me in the day of trouble: I will deliver thee, and thou shalt glorify me."[30]

3. What is intercession?

Following supplications and prayers, we are to make intercession for all those in authority as well as all others. Intercession is temporarily restraining Satan's influence in another person's life so that they are free to respond to God's truth.

Jesus interceded for Simon Peter at a time when He knew that Satan's influence over Peter's life was dangerously imminent. "And the Lord said, Simon, Simon, behold, Satan hath desired to have you, that he may sift you as wheat: But I have prayed for thee, that thy faith fail not: and when thou art converted, strengthen thy brethren."[31]

Intercession is also placing a "hedge of protection" around a Godly person's life so that Satan cannot bring any damage or defeat. When Satan wanted to destroy Job, Satan complained about the "hedge" that God had placed around Job's life and all of his possessions.

"Then Satan answered the LORD, and said, Doth Job fear God for nought? Hast not thou made an hedge about him, and about his house, and about all that he hath on every side? thou hast blessed the work of his hands, and his substance is increased in the land."[32]

God continually looks for righteous believers who will intercede for their people and their land. "And I sought for a man among them, that should make up the hedge, and stand in the gap before me for the land, that I should not destroy it: but I found none."[33]

The New Testament concept of the hedge can be seen in such analogies as the hen gathering her chickens under her wings,[34] or the shepherd building a protective wall around the sheep and then blocking the door so no wolves, lions, or bears can get in to attack the sheep.[35]

Intercession is also asking God to place a "hedge of thorns" around one who is outside of God's will. The purpose of such a hedge is to discourage and drive away all wrong influences in that person's life, including spiritual influences and wrong friends.

God gives a beautiful picture of a "hedge of thorns" in the account of Hosea and Gomer. Hosea married Gomer, but she became a rebellious, immoral wife. She went out after many other lovers and desecrated the sanctity of the marriage into which she had entered. Therefore, Hosea asked God to place around her a "hedge of thorns."

The result of this hedge would be threefold. First, she would be confused, because a double-minded person is unstable in all his ways;[36] second, her adulterous lovers would lose interest in her and leave; and third, she would decide to return to her husband. Here is the account:

"Therefore, behold, I will hedge up thy way with thorns, and make a wall, that she shall not find her paths. And she shall follow after her lovers, but she shall not overtake them; and she shall seek them, but shall not find them: then shall she say, I will go and return to my first husband; for then was it better with me than now."[37]

One of the great intercessors in Scripture was Samuel. He understood the importance and effectiveness of intercession when he said, "Moreover as for me, God forbid that I should sin against the LORD in ceasing to pray for you: but I will teach you the good and the right way."[38]

God instructs us to pray for all in authority for several important reasons, including the reason that leaders and their families are under special temptation and pressures because of their public responsibilities. They are also judged by a higher standard than those under them.

TEN DANGERS THAT CAUSE LEADERS TO FALL

A leader will be more susceptible to the following temptations. If he falls, those under his jurisdiction will experience greater temptations and any consequences of the leader's failure. This fact should be a strong motivation for believers to pray for all their authorities.

1. *Pride*—Pride is believing that we achieved what in reality God and others have done for us and through us. Pride results when we build all of life around ourselves and refuse to honor God as God. It is reserving the right to make final decisions rather than humbly seeking God for His wisdom and direction in every matter.

2. *Fear of Man*—The fear of man brings a snare.[39] This leads to gaining the praise of man by compromises rather than doing what is right in the fear of the Lord. God asks, "Who art thou, that thou shouldest be afraid of a man that shall die, and of the son of man which shall be made as grass; And forgettest the LORD thy maker, that hath stretched

forth the heavens, and laid the foundations of the earth. . . ?"[40]

3. *Unwise Advisers*—It is not the leader who has the most influence but those who advise the leader. Evil or unwise advisers give counsel based on selfish motives or human reasoning rather than on God's wisdom. When Solomon's son became king, he forsook the counsel of the wise, older men that stood before his father and followed the unwise counsel of his peers with whom he had grown up. Heeding this unwise counsel cost him most of the kingdom.[41]

4. *Showing Partiality in Judgment*—It is the responsibility of leaders to defend the poor, fatherless, widows, and strangers from the oppression of the rich.[42] Those who searched for Jesus could usually find Him among the poor. God gives severe warnings about neglecting the poor in order to favor the rich. The rich who oppress, as well as others who participate with them, will experience calamities.[43]

5. *Not Promptly Dealing With Problems*—A leader is given special authority to deal with problems, *if* he begins to act upon them in the day he hears of them.[44] A neglect to deal with problems gives the message to others that they are not important, and thus encourages the problems to be enlarged and repeated.

6. *Love of Money*—Scripture identifies the love of money as "the root of all evil."[45] It makes the leader vulnerable to greed and bribes, which "blindeth the wise, and perverteth the words of the righteous."[46] Money can become an idol when we expect from it that which only God can give, such as security, joy, and peace. Money gained by means that damage the

lives of others, such as liquor and drugs, carries a curse with it.[47]

7. *Lust and Immorality*—Lust can be physical or mental adultery. This is one of the greatest traps to a leader. Lusting after women was the downfall of the purest, strongest, and wisest leaders who ever lived.

8. *Rejection of Critics*—Critics point to our blind spots and keep us aware of our daily need for God's wisdom and protection. An unwise leader is unapproachable for criticism and then experiences the consequences of failing to see important situations through the eyes of other people.

9. *Wrong Priorities*—The first priority of a leader must be his own personal walk with the Lord. The kings of Israel were commanded to make their own personal copy of the Law, so it would be their daily companion. A leader's marriage and family must be his second priority. If he fails to govern his own house, how can he effectively govern the affairs of others?[48] A leader's third priority is his work responsibility.

10. *Retirement Focus*—Working toward a retirement of ease is neither healthy nor appropriate for a leader. He tends to lose his awareness of ongoing warfare and surrenders opportunities for achievement that are often experienced near the end of the race. During his elderly years, David conquered giants,[49] Caleb conquered a mountain,[50] and John recorded glorious truths.[51] God's only retirement program is Heaven.

4. What is involved in giving of thanks?

After praying and interceding for leaders, it is important to give thanks for them and for God's working through them to accomplish His will and work in the world. There are four structures of authority that God recognizes. Each one is responsible for a specific area of jurisdiction that affects our lives.

1. Family authority[52]
2. Government authority[53]
3. Church authority[54]
4. Employment authority[55]

In giving thanks for those whom God has placed over us, it is good to list the various ways they have benefited our lives. The following list can be used as a guide during our times of thanksgiving before the Lord:[56]

- For peace that comes under wise leadership
- For civil leaders as "ministers of God"
- For public utilities and community order
- For the protection of law officers
- For spiritual care from church leaders
- For the diligence of company founders

Giving thanks must be a continual activity for the believer, based on the instruction of God: "In every thing give thanks: for this is the will of God in Christ Jesus concerning you."[57]

THE IMPORTANCE OF POSITIONS IN PRAYER

Though prayer can be given from any position, Scripture does identify several specific positions. We can understand from the context of Scripture the significance of each one..

1. Falling on my face before God

This position demonstrates a sense of total unworthiness and inadequacy before God. It expresses the kind of humility and fear of the Lord that God honors. "[Abraham] fell on his face" before God,[58] and the man with leprosy "fell on his face" when he saw Jesus and said, "Lord, if thou wilt, thou canst make me clean."[59]

2. Kneeling before the Lord

Kneeling is an expression of worship and reverence. One day every knee shall bow and every tongue shall confess that Jesus Christ is Lord, to the glory of God the Father.[60]

Kneeling is also an expression of earnest appeal. The rich young ruler knelt down and asked Jesus what he must do to inherit eternal life,[61] and Solomon knelt down to ask God for His blessing on the Temple that he and the people had built.[62] The Psalmist prayed, "O come, let us worship and bow down: let us kneel before the Lord our maker."[63]

3. Bowing before the Lord

Bowing before a person is a sign of honor and respect. It acknowledges the worth and importance of the person being bowed to. When the nation of Israel gathered before the Lord, "the king and all that were present with him bowed themselves, and worshipped."[64]

4. Standing before the Lord

Standing signifies a position of responsibility and delegated authority. When Joseph was thirty years old, he "stood before Pharaoh" in a position of responsibility.[65] When we stand before the Lord in prayer, we are not able to stand in our own righteousness but only in the righteousness of Jesus Christ.

Standing is also related to spiritual warfare. "Wherefore take unto you the whole armour of God, that ye may be able to withstand in the evil day, and having done all, to stand. Stand therefore, having your loins girt about with truth, and having on the breastplate of righteousness."[66]

5. Looking up to Heaven

Looking up in prayer is possible only when a person is in full fellowship with the Lord and has a clear conscience. If there is any sin in his life, it will be hard for a person to look up into the face of Jesus, in the same way that it is hard for a guilty person to look into the eyes of his earthly authorities.

Looking up also symbolizes recognition of God as the source of our strength, direction, and provision in order to do His will. When Jesus took the bread and fish, "He looked up to heaven, and blessed."[67] When Stephen was in the council "he, being full of the Holy Ghost, looked up stedfastly into heaven, and saw the glory of God, and Jesus standing on the right hand of God."[68]

6. Stretching forth the arm

The power and authority that come from stretching forth the arm are confirmed in both the Old and New Testaments. Stretching forth the arm is an action against the forces of evil and carries with it the testimony of God's power and victory.

This position is symbolized by Moses and Joshua. When Moses held up his hands during the war with Amalek, Israel prevailed;[69] when he put his hands down, Amalek prevailed. When Joshua faced the city of Ai in battle, God told him that when he stretched forth his hand with a spear in it, He would give him the city.[70]

Fourteen times in Scripture God relates His deliverance during conflict to "the stretched out arm."

- "I will redeem you with a stretched out arm, and with great judgments."[71]

- The Lord took Israel from the midst of Egypt by an outstretched arm. "Thou broughtest [them] out by thy mighty power and by thy stretched out arm."[72]

- God even used an outstretched arm in creating the heavens and the earth. "Ah Lord GOD! behold, thou hast made the heaven and the earth by thy great power and stretched out arm, and there is nothing too hard for thee."[73]

- The prophet Ezekiel related the rule of God to an outstretched arm. "As I live, saith the Lord GOD, surely with a mighty hand, and with a stretched out arm, and with fury poured out, will I rule over you."[74]

- Fear of the enemy can be conquered by remembering the power of the outstretched arm. "The mighty hand, and the stretched out arm, whereby the LORD thy God brought thee out: so shall the LORD thy God do unto all the people of whom thou art afraid."[75]

- Solomon stretched forth his hands throughout his prayer of dedication for the Temple, and concluded his prayer with a blessing to the people.[76]

In the New Testament, Paul emphasizes the importance of "stretching forth the arm" with holiness, forgiveness, and faith. "I will therefore that men pray every where, lifting up holy hands, without wrath and doubting."[77]

There are three qualifications for effective prayer in this passage. The first is "lifting up holy hands." This would certainly relate to a clear conscience and a pure heart as further defined by James: "Draw nigh to God, and he will draw nigh to you. Cleanse your hands, ye sinners; and purify your hearts, ye double-minded."[78]

The second requirement is to pray "without wrath." This requires forgiveness of all who offend us, because wrath and bitterness defile a person and make his prayers ineffective.[79]

The third requirement is to pray in faith without "doubting." This would refer to the rhemas in Scripture that God has given to a person, which he can use as the basis of his prayers. "If ye abide in me, and my words [*rhema*] abide in you, ye shall ask what ye will, and it shall be done unto you."[80]

THE POWER OF PRAYING "IN JESUS' NAME"

Jesus repeatedly emphasized that "if ye shall ask any thing in my name, I will do it."[81] This does not mean that we simply attach Jesus' name to the end of our prayers, but that we base our prayers on what His name represents.

For example, God tells us to not worry about the future. We can therefore pray for inward peace in the name of Jesus, Who is the Prince of Peace.[82] We can pray for the healing of our soul, because Jesus is the Great Physician.[83] Jesus said, "Hitherto have ye asked nothing in my name: ask, and ye shall receive, that your joy may be full."[84] Therefore, we should learn the names of God and view them as signatures on blank checks.

THE KEY TO PRAYING WITH POWER

The term *one accord*[85] is the key to effective corporate prayer. It comes from two Greek words which mean "at the same place or time" and "passion." It is used almost exclusively in the Book of Acts to describe the believers' praying with power. Thus if anyone in the group is in disharmony, they disrupt the potential of powerful prayer.[86]

Notes

1. Acts 4:31.
2. I Corinthians 1:2.
3. I Timothy 3:15.
4. Hebrews 12:23.
5. Revelation 2:1.
6. Matthew 21:13.
7. Mark 11:17.
8. I Corinthians 12:26.
9. Galatians 6:10.
10. Ephesians 6:18.
11. Ephesians 3:14–21.
12. I Timothy 2:1–4.
13. Ibid.
14. I Timothy 2:1.
15. Deuteronomy 28:64.
16. II Chronicles 7:14.
17. Daniel 9:17–19.
18. James 4:3.
19. Nehemiah 1–2.
20. II Kings 19:15–19.
21. Romans 8:27, Luke 4:3–14.
22. Matthew 7:8.
23. Ephesians 6:12.
24. Matthew 18:19.
25. Matthew 6:18.
26. Isaiah 58:8–11, Psalm 37:6.
27. II Corinthians 12:8–9.
28. I Thessalonians 5:17.
29. Luke 18:1–8.
30. Psalm 50:15.
31. Luke 22:31–32.
32. Job 1:9–10.
33. Ezekiel 22:30.
34. Matthew 23:37.
35. John 10:7–15.
36. James 1:8.
37. Hosea 2:6–7.
38. I Samuel 12:23.
39. Proverbs 29:25.
40. Isaiah 51:12–13.
41. I Kings 12:8.
42. Zechariah 7:10.
43. James 5:1.
44. Numbers 30:3–5.
45. I Timothy 6:10.
46. Exodus 23:8.
47. Proverbs 28:8.
48. I Timothy 3:5.
49. I Chronicles 20:8.
50. Deuteronomy 1:36.
51. Revelation 1:9–10.
52. Ephesians 6:1–3.
53. Romans 13:1–7.
54. I Timothy 5:17.
55. Colossians 3:22–23.
56. I Timothy 2:1–4.
57. I Thessalonians 5:18.
58. Genesis 17:1–4.
59. Luke 5:12.
60. Philippians 2:10–11.
61. Mark 10:17.
62. I Kings 8:54.
63. Psalm 95:6.
64. II Chronicles 29:29.
65. Genesis 41:46.
66. Ephesians 6:13–14.
67. Mark 6:41.
68. Acts 7:55.
69. Exodus 17:11–12.
70. Joshua 8:18, Joshua 8:26.
71. Exodus 6:6.
72. Deuteronomy 9:29.
73. Jeremiah 32:17.
74. Ezekiel 20:33.
75. Deuteronomy 7:19.
76. I Kings 8:22–61.
77. I Timothy 2:8.
78. James 4:8.
79. Hebrews 12:15.
80. John 15:7.
81. John 14:14.
82. Isaiah 9:6.
83. Exodus 15:26.
84. John 16:24.
85. James Strong, S.T.D., LL.D, *Strong's Exhaustive Concordance of the Bible*, McDonald Publishing Company, McClean, Virginia, #3661.
86. Acts 1:14; 2:1, 4:24.

A good work takes place when the leaders whom we serve get the credit, God gets the glory, and we have the joy of lasting fruit.

"Let your light so shine before men, that they may see your good works, and glorify your Father which is in heaven."

—Matthew 5:16

THE POWER OF ITS SERVICE

Chapter Summary

*I*n the same way that sincere prayer is universally appreciated, genuine service to people in need is universally respected. It is not surprising, therefore, that God redeemed every believer to be zealous of good works as a means of demonstrating Christ's love and earning a hearing for the good news of the Gospel. The common refrain of the world is, "We don't care how much you know until we know how much you care." Believers tend to bypass good works to tell people about their faith, but God's order is just the opposite. First, let men see your good works, and then they will be ready to hear your good words. Indeed, good works are powerful, but when leaders get the credit for those good works, their effectiveness multiplies.

The evidence of the power of love among believers in the first-century Church was their common sharing of resources with each other. The evidence of their love to those outside the Church was the carrying out of good works to the glory of God.

How Good Works Follow Fervent Prayer

It is not possible to pray for all men—especially all those in authority—and not be exposed to significant opportunities to do good works.

Leaders are usually looking for help with the following needs:

1. Strengthening or rebuilding their marriages
2. Counseling rebellious sons and daughters
3. Direction to gain financial freedom
4. Information on solving health problems

To give assistance and help in these areas presupposes that Biblical and proven answers have been searched out and can be clearly and effectively explained.

When Jesus began His public ministry, He opened the Book of Isaiah and read the following passage:

"The spirit of the Lord GOD is upon me; because the LORD hath anointed me to preach good tidings unto the meek; he hath sent me to bind up the brokenhearted, to proclaim liberty to the captives, and the opening of the prison to them that are bound; To proclaim the acceptable year of the LORD."[1]

This was the ministry of Jesus, and He has sent us to follow in His steps; therefore these ought to be our goals as well. It is for this purpose that the Holy Spirit has been given to us. "Then said Jesus to them again, Peace be unto you: as my Father hath sent me, even so send I you. And when he had said this, he breathed on them, and saith unto them, Receive ye the Holy Ghost."[2]

How Believers Were Designed for Good Works

Believers were designed to carry out good works. "For we are his workmanship, created in

Christ Jesus unto good works, which God hath before ordained that we should walk in them."[3] It may be surprising for many believers to realize that they were not only created for good works but that this is the mark of true Christianity. Jesus "gave himself for us, that he might redeem us from all iniquity, and purify unto himself a peculiar people, zealous of good works."[4]

We all have a natural inclination to seek personal comfort or use our energy to serve ourselves. It takes creative thinking and consistent urging to go against this tendency in order to accomplish good works. This is the calling and responsibility of every believer. "And let us consider one another to provoke unto love and to good works."[5]

Good works are also an expression of wisdom and a demonstration of faith. "Who is a wise man and endued with knowledge among you? let him shew out of a good conversation his works with meekness of wisdom."[6]

In order for good works to be effective, they must be carried out by Godly believers who are living in personal purity with a good conscience. "If a man therefore purge himself from these, he shall be a vessel unto honour, sanctified, and meet for the master's use, and prepared unto every good work."[7]

The job description of a believer is not in terms of a lifelong profession, but in an ever-expanding outreach through good works. As a benediction to the vital importance of good works, God gives us the following passage: May He "make you perfect in every good work to do his will, working in you that which is well-pleasing in his sight, through Jesus Christ; to whom be glory for ever and ever. Amen."[8]

What Constitutes a Good Work?

A good work is initiated by the Holy Spirit in response to a need. A good work does not draw attention or praise to the one doing it but rather to others so that in honor, we prefer one another. Since leaders are the ministers of God for doing good and since we are to pray for all those in authority, it follows that our good works should bring honor to them.

Jesus emphasized the benefit of good works before good words when He said, "Let your light so shine before men, that they may see your good works, and glorify your Father which is in heaven."[9] The reward of a good work comes when it is done in such a way that gives others the credit and God the glory.

When we give, we are to give in secret. God promises that if we do this, He will reward us openly with the lasting fruit that comes from that good work.[10] By doing good works and deflecting the praise to others, we are fulfilling the Biblical instruction of "preferring one another" in honor.[11]

How to "Do Good Unto All"

Scripture instructs us to "do good unto all men."[12] That sounds like an impossible task. Yet it does become possible as we serve those who are in authority. For example, by praying for and serving the mayor of a city and helping him do good to all those under his jurisdiction, we are, in effect, serving all.

Focusing on service to the leaders of cities, states, and nations is very appropriate, as Scripture refers to them as ministers of God who are given the primary function of doing good to those under their jurisdictions. "For rulers are not a terror to good works . . . . For he is the minister of God to thee for good."[13] Our service to them should be to help them do good, which would also aid them in fulfilling their God-given responsibility.

The Word of God gives clear examples of serving the needs of cities. Job was the most Godly and righteous man of his day. His account of caring for the poor of the land assumes that God's judgment would have been upon him had he not done it.

"If I have withheld the poor from their desire, or have caused the eyes of the widow to fail; Or have eaten my morsel myself alone, and the fatherless hath not eaten thereof; (For from my youth he was brought up with me, as with a father, and I have guided her from my mother's womb;) If I have seen any perish for want of clothing, or any poor without covering;

"If his loins have not blessed me, and if he were not warmed with the fleece of my sheep; If I have lifted up my hand against the fatherless, when I saw my help in the gate: Then let mine arm fall from my shoulder blade, and mine arm be broken from the bone."[14]

God gives us a significant axiom about who is to benefit when He prospers a righteous person. "When it goeth well with the righteous, the city rejoiceth."[15] Notice that God did not say his family rejoices, or the church rejoices, but that the city rejoices. This could only be true if the city directly benefited from his prosperity. This point is further emphasized by the following Scripture: "By the blessing of the upright the city is exalted."[16]

This emphasis on serving all the people of the city is seen in the first-century Church under the most adverse conditions possible. The Roman government had just killed Jesus. The religious authorities were envious of the Church, and they were doing all they could to destroy it. Under the authority of those leaders, Saul later made havoc of the Church.[17]

In spite of opposition, the apostles went throughout the city doing good. They freely healed and delivered those in need. "Insomuch that they brought forth the sick into the streets, and laid them on beds and couches, that at the least the shadow of Peter passing by might overshadow some of them.

"There came also a multitude out of the cities round about unto Jerusalem, bringing sick folks, and them which were vexed with unclean spirits: and they were healed every one."[18]

The very rulers that attacked the New Testament Church were identified by Paul as ministers of God for doing good.

Peter suffered an excruciating death at the hands of civil government,[19] yet he also affirmed the importance of being under their authority, doing good works to glorify God.

"Having your conversation honest among the Gentiles: that, whereas they speak against you as evildoers, they may by your good works, which they shall behold, glorify God in the day of visitation.

"Submit yourselves to every ordinance of man for the Lord's sake: whether it be to the king, as supreme; Or unto governors, as unto them that are sent by him for the punishment of evildoers, and for the praise of them that do well. For so is the will of God, that with well-doing ye may put to silence the ignorance of foolish men."[20]

Several years ago, a local church followed this principle. They went to the mayor of their rural town and explained that they were going to be taking baskets of food to poor families in the area and would like to do so as an expression of caring concern from his office.

They asked if he would write a little note of encouragement, which would be placed in each basket. They also assured him that there would be no promotional material from their church. The mayor agreed to this plan, and the baskets were purchased and distributed by the believers.

The surprised recipients began calling the mayor's office and thanking him for his thoughtfulness and generosity in caring for their needs.

As the next Thanksgiving approached, the mayor called the pastor and asked if he was going to do it again. The pastor said that he would like to, and the mayor enthusiastically replied, "That's good, because I have contacted some supermarkets, and they are going to provide all the food without charge."

Meanwhile, the mayor asked the pastor if he would be willing to meet a particular need in their community. Thousands of migrant workers were living in the area, and the city government was being required to provide the training that was needed for them to learn to speak English. Would he and the church do the training? The pastor asked if he could use the Bible as their English textbook—the mayor said that would be fine.

When somebody now asks this pastor in a small, rural community how many are in his church, he replies, "About three thousand."[21]

The action of this church motivated the leader to see the importance of good works within his community and to honor those who were per-forming them.

Actually, God gave the church the responsi-bility of carrying out the social needs of the com-munity. The early Church assumed the responsibility of caring for their widows.[22] By default, the gov-ernment now has this responsibility. However, as believers become zealous of good works, the Biblical pattern can be restored.

THE PRINCIPLE OF SERVING UNDER AUTHORITY

If we want to serve someone, we must first get under that person's authority; otherwise, our service will not be accepted or appreciated.

Jesus himself illustrates this principle. When He left the splendor of Heaven for His earthly ministry, He was "registered" by the Roman government in their official census, the very government that later put Him on the cross.[23]

Jesus also instructed His disciples to carry out this principle when He sent them out to every city to which He Himself would go. He said, "And into whatsoever city or town ye shall enter, inquire who in it is worthy; and there abide till ye go thence. And when ye come into an house, salute it. And if the house be worthy, let your peace come upon it."[24]

Although the "worthy one" is not specifically identified, his rejection of the disciples resulted in the dust of the city being shaken off their feet. This would indicate that the "worthy one" was in a representative position, because the entire city would be affected.[25] The word *worthy* comes from the Greek word *axios*,[26] which probably has its root in the Greek word *ago*,[27] which means "to lead."

The most obvious worthy one of the city would be the one whom the people elected to lead them. The disciples were to remain in his house as long as they were in the city. From there, they were to carry out good works and preach the Gospel. Since they were under the authority of the worthy one, those who were helped would express gratefulness to this person and give glory to God.

God does not expect every leader to be open to the offer of good works or receive those who come with that purpose. He made provision for this possibility in His further instruction to His disciples. "But if it be not worthy, let your peace return to you. And whosoever shall not receive you, nor hear your words, when ye depart out of that house or city, shake off the dust of your feet."[28]

The principle of getting under authority is effective at every level of service. A few years ago, several hundred sincere, Christian young people went into a low-income neighborhood designated by the city of Indianapolis as a needy community.

The enthusiastic young people began knocking on doors. They explained that the mayor had invited them to provide free service to the community and that they would be willing to do any work that was needed, such as raking leaves, fixing gutters, repairing front porches, painting, or hauling away trash.

Surprisingly, these low-income, needy people refused the help. They replied, "No, thank you. We are doing just fine!"

Finally, one of the young people applied the principle of serving under authority and received an entirely different response. The young person said, "The mayor has invited us to serve in this community, but we really do not know how to go about doing it. Would you give us counsel on what we could do to be of help?"

They were warmly welcomed into the home and told about a widow down the street who was unable to fix her gutters and would certainly appreciate their help.

The widow was delighted and grateful. When she thanked the young people, they deflected the praise to the mayor and the neighbors who had directed them to her. This "new approach" involved a humble spirit—"Would you help us?"—rather than a proud spirit—"We are here to help you—you poor, incapable people."

Within a year of this new approach, the doors of the community opened. The city made this group of young people honorary members of the community, and lasting spiritual fruit has resulted from their service.[29]

Several months before this successful service, a well-known Christian organization singled out this particular community for door-to-door evangelism. After all their door-to-door outreach, they concluded that this was the hardest, most resistant neighborhood they had ever worked in. One pastor in this community explained the hardness to the Gospel by relating the following incident. "I and my deacon knocked on every door on block after block. The people were home, but no one would even answer the door."

Daniel provides another example of this principle. He was one of the captives who was carried to Babylon and selected to serve the king. His "registration" included being given a new name, Belteshazzar. When it came to violating Scripture, however, he refused to do so and was instead willing to go to the lions' den.[30]

Is the Church to Serve or to Be Served?

Jesus clearly stated that He did not come to be served but to serve. He taught and demonstrated this principle by explaining that "whosoever will be great among you, shall be your minister: And whosoever of you will be the chiefest, shall be servant of all. For even the Son of man came not to be ministered unto, but to minister, and to give his life a ransom for many."[31]

It follows, then, that Christ's Church should not be the object of service but the "headquarters" from which to serve the entire community.

There is a strong emphasis today for pastors to build their churches. Yet as the first-century Christians demonstrated genuine love to each other and to all the people in the community, the Lord built His Church. "And believers were the more added to the Lord, multitudes both of men and women."[32]

If the major emphasis of a church is to increase its attendance in church programs, the public leaders will develop a resistance against any offers for help. They will assume that the church has an ulterior motive for serving them and that the church is simply using the leaders of the community to advance its own program.

Genuine love does not have any personal agenda. Its sole desire is to give to the needs of others, without any motive of personal reward.

A pastor in Oklahoma City asked his state legislator how he and members of his church could serve their community. The legislator gave him a test by suggesting that they pick up litter around the neighborhood. They fulfilled this task and directed back to the legislator any praise they received for it. This resulted in other opportunities for the pastor to minister in the community.

For years, they had been trying to reach the students in the public school across the street. However, it was a closed door to them. Then one day, the pastor talked to the school officials and asked how he could serve them. They expressed a need for trained Character Coaches to teach a character curriculum to their students.

The pastor had some of the outstanding young people in his church trained to do this, and it was well received by the school. The Character Coaches were not able to present the Gospel. However, during the following summer, special youth programs were planned and many of the young people attended them and learned how they could establish a personal relationship with God through the Lord Jesus Christ.[33]

For the last five years, hundreds of mayors, governors, and leaders of other nations have been drawn to a three-day conference to learn how the youths and parents in their cities and nations can become like the youths and families who have been serving in this way during the past ten years. Traditional barriers of culture, language, age, race, economics, and religion are being broken down by the genuine love being demonstrated to these leaders. The Head of the Department of Education of Moscow, Russia, stated to a group of these committed believers several years ago: "Many armies have tried to conquer our nation and failed. However, you have conquered us with love."[34] A member of the Young Men's Communist Association of China visited our headquarters and exclaimed, "We recognize that you have sincere love, and we would like you to bring your work over to our country."[35] Truly, the greatest force on the face of the earth is genuine love.[36]

Notes

1. Isaiah 61:1–2.
2. John 20:21–22.
3. Ephesians 2:10.
4. Titus 2:14.
5. Hebrews 10:24.
6. James 3:13.
7. II Timothy 2:21.
8. Hebrews 13:21.
9. Matthew 5:16.
10. Matthew 6:4.
11. Romans 12:10.
12. Galatians 6:10.
13. Romans 13:3–4.
14. Job 31:16–22.
15. Proverbs 11:10.
16. Proverbs 11:11.
17. Acts 8:3.
18. Acts 5:15–16.
19. John 21:18–19.
20. I Peter 2:12–15.
21. Public testimony given at an All-Day Ministers' Seminar.
22. Acts 6–7.
23. Luke 2:1–5.
24. Matthew 10:11–13.
25. The parallel passage in Luke 10 states that the city rejected the disciples.
26. James Strong, S.T.D., LL.D, *Strong's Exhaustive Concordance of the Bible*, McDonald Publishing Company, McClean, Virginia, #514.
27. James Strong, S.T.D., LL.D, *Strong's Exhaustive Concordance of the Bible*, McDonald Publishing Company, McClean, Virginia, #71.
28. Matthew 10:13–14.
29. Fountain Square Outreach 1993, IBLP Staff and Volunteers.
30. Daniel 1, 6.
31. Mark 10:43–45.
32. Acts 5:14.
33. Rev. Jerry Wells, Oklahoma City, OK.
34. Dr. Loubov Kezina, Head of the Department of Education for the city of Moscow, Russia.
35. A visitor from Beijing, China.
36. I Corinthians 13.

Appendix

ADDITIONAL INFORMATION

What Is Genuine Love?

How Confirming Testimonies Resulted
in a Tenfold Increase in Conversions

How a Father Led His Family in First-
Century-Type Worship

A character hymnbook is being prepared for use in first-century-type churches. It will include forty-nine character qualities with Biblical definitions. After each quality there will be related hymns, songs, and hymn histories. Here is an example of one definition:

LOVE vs. Selfishness

LOVE IS GIVING TO THE BASIC NEEDS OF OTHERS SO THAT THEIR AUTHORITIES GET THE CREDIT, GOD GETS THE GLORY, AND WE HAVE THE JOY OF ETERNAL REWARDS.

The Biblical Terms for Love

The primary Greek words for love are *agapao* and *phileo*. Agapao means "to welcome, to entertain, to be fond of, to love dearly, to be well pleased, to be content." On the other hand, *phileo* refers to a fondness or friendship. (The Greek word *philanthropia* is a "fondness of mankind, benevolence, and love towards others.") Another Greek word for love is *philadelphia*, which means "fraternal affection, brotherly love and kindness."

When Jesus asked Peter if he loved Him, Jesus used the stronger of these words—*agapao*, but Peter responded with the weaker term—*phileo*. "Jesus saith to Simon Peter, Simon, son of Jonas, lovest [*agapao*] thou me more than these? He saith unto him, Yea, Lord; thou knowest that I love [*phileo*] thee. He saith unto him, Feed my lambs.

"He saith to him again the second time, Simon, son of Jonas, lovest [*agapao*] thou me? He saith unto him, Yea, Lord; thou knowest that I love [*phileo*] thee. He saith unto him, Feed my sheep. He saith unto him the third time, Simon, son of Jonas, lovest [*phileo*] thou me?

Peter was grieved because he said unto him the third time, Lovest [*phileo*] thou me? And he said unto him, Lord, thou knowest all things; thou knowest that I love [*phileo*] thee" (John 21:15–17).

Jesus then told Peter about the suffering he would experience. If we respond to suffering with joy and thankfulness, we receive the power of the Holy Spirit with agape love; therefore, it is through suffering that our love is perfected and deepened. (See II Corinthians 12:9.) Twenty-eight times in the New Testament the Greek word *agape* is translated "charity."

How Light Explains the True Expression of Love

In John's epistle on love, he explains that "God is light" (I John 1:5) and "God is love" (I John 4:8). The significance of equating light and love is that neither one determines who will benefit from its service. All who come to the light receive its benefits, regardless of their spiritual condition. Similarly, all who come to us should receive the benefit of God's love through us.

God loves everyone in the world so much that He gave His only begotten Son as full payment for our sin, in order that whosoever believes on Him and receives Him as their substitute will receive the power to become the sons of God and have eternal life. (See John 3:16, John 1:12.)

How Genuine Love Is Demonstrated by Giving

Each time Peter stated that he loved Jesus, Jesus told him to give to the basic needs of others. "Feed my lambs," "Feed my sheep," and "Feed my sheep." (See John 21:15–17.) Our motivation in giving to fellow believers is that we are actually giving to Jesus. "Inasmuch as ye have done it unto one of the least of these my brethren, ye have done it unto me" (Matthew 25:40).

Love is not complete without giving. "God so loved the world, that he gave . . ." (John 3:16). If we see a person in obvious need and say to him, "Be clothed or be warmed," but do not give to his need, "how dwelleth the love of God in [us]?" (See I John 3:17.)

Love will manifest itself in generous giving through good works. If these are done with pure motives and credit is given to others, God will be glorified. Therefore, we are commanded, "Let your light so shine before men, that they may see your good works, and glorify your Father which is in heaven" (Matthew 5:16).

First-century believers had such powerful love that they claimed nothing as their own but sold their goods and gave the money to care for the needs of other believers. (See Acts 4:32–35.)

The Vital Importance of Love

Genuine love is the most important of all character qualities. Every other quality must be motivated by it, or the quality will be empty and of no benefit. "Though I bestow all my goods to feed the poor [kindness, compassion, and generosity], and though I give my body to be burned [sincerity, courage, and determination], and have not charity, it profiteth me nothing" (I Corinthians 13:3).

Agape love is greater than faith and hope (see I Corinthians 13:13). It is the greatest commandment given by God (see Matthew 22:36–40). It is the credential of a true local church (see Revelation 1:20–2:5). and the badge of a true disciple (see John 13:35). It is the primary request of Jesus in His final prayer for His disciples (see John 17).

God's Description of Love

Because love is so important and there are many distorted ideas of what it is, God devoted an entire chapter in I Corinthians to define exactly what it involves.

1. Love suffereth long.

It does not lose heart. It perseveres with patience and bravely endures misfortunes and troubles. It bears offenses and injuries with joy and confidence that a good reward will come from the hand of God.

153

Qualities: endurance, patience, forgiveness, joyfulness, faith, loyalty, flexibility

2. Love is kind.

It looks for ways to be useful and acts benevolently. It is easy to be entreated and has the motivation of giving rather than taking. It focuses on people's needs rather than their faults.

Qualities: kindness, generosity, availability, creativity, compassion, sensitivity, initiative, gentleness, alertness

3. Love envieth not.

It does not boil with desires to have that which belongs to others. It is not possessive of what has been entrusted to it. It is content with basic necessities and rich fellowship with the Lord.

Qualities: gratefulness, contentment, resourcefulness, thriftiness, security

4. Love vaunteth not itself.

It does not boast of its abilities or its accomplishments. It does not look for ways to promote itself or extol its virtues with rhetorical embellishments.

Qualities: sincerity, meekness, deference

5. Love is not puffed up.

It does not cherish exaggerated ideas of its own importance. It does not look down on others with contempt or disdain. It is not proud.

Qualities: virtue, humility

6. Love doth not behave itself unseemly.

It does not flaunt itself to attract attention or to stir up sensual desires in others. It does not act indecently or shamefully. It has good manners.

Qualities: self-control, discretion, responsibility

7. Love seeketh not her own.

It does not demand its own way. It does not crave things for its own pleasure or profit. It does not focus on itself but on the needs of others. It is willing to lay down its life for the benefit of others.

Qualities: hospitality, dependability

8. Love is not easily provoked.

It does not get irritated or exasperated. It conquers anger and wrath. It is not quickly excited to rivalry but rather to helping others succeed.

Qualities: reverence, cautiousness, punctuality, orderliness

9. Love thinketh no evil.

It guards its heart and mind and brings every thought into captivity to the obedience of Christ. It distinguishes between good and evil and rejects the evil. It does not retain wrong desires or plans or harbor hurtful feelings toward others.

Qualities: obedience, thoroughness, discernment

10. Love rejoices not in iniquity.

It grieves when evil people are promoted and unjust laws are made. It does not secretly desire to carry out the lusts of the flesh, the lusts of the eyes, or the prideful goals of life.

Qualities: justice, decisiveness, determination

11. Love rejoices in the truth.

It delights in God's Law and meditates on it day and night. It dwells upon thoughts that are true, honest, just, pure, lovely, and of a good report. It is eager to share truth with others and rejoices with all good people when truth prevails.

Qualities: truthfulness, boldness, persuasiveness, diligence, enthusiasm, attentiveness, wisdom

This kind of love "beareth all things, believeth all things, hopeth all things, endureth all things." It can outlast anything, because love "never faileth" (I Corinthians 13:7–8).

How Love Is Developed

The power of genuine love is a reward of being in fellowship with God's Holy Spirit and successfully passing the tests that He designs for our spiritual growth. When a person becomes a believer by faith in the finished work of the Lord Jesus Christ, the Holy Spirit indwells his spirit. Each believer can then ask his Heavenly Father to fill his soul with the Holy Spirit based on the promise of Luke 11:13. "If ye then, being evil, know how to give good gifts unto your children: how much more shall your heavenly Father give the Holy Spirit to them that ask him?"

The Holy Spirit will then take the believer through times of testing. If the believer responds with rejoicing and gratefulness, a powerful spirit of love will come upon him. This sequence is seen throughout the New Testament, beginning with the life of Jesus. After He was filled with the Spirit (Luke 4:1), the Spirit immediately led Him into the wilderness for testing, and He returned—not in the fullness of the Spirit, but in the power of the Spirit. (See Luke 4:1–14.)

In the same way, the Thessalonian believers received the Holy Spirit at their conversion. Then they endured "much affliction, with joy of the Holy Ghost" (I Thessalonians 1:6). The result was that their faith grew exceedingly and their love for each other abounded. (See II Thessalonians 1:3–4.) This is the pattern described by Paul: "We glory in tribulations also: knowing that tribulation worketh patience; And patience, experience; and experience, hope: And hope maketh not ashamed; because the love of God is shed abroad in our hearts by the Holy Ghost which is given unto us" (Romans 5:1–5).

156

How Genuine Is Your Love?

- Do you tend to get discouraged and want to give up when everything seems to go wrong?
- Do you look for ways to be useful and help out wherever you go?
- Do you tend to envy the possessions or opportunities of other people?
- Do you enjoy telling about your achievements more than listening to the accomplishments of others?
- Do you tend to look down on those who do not live by your standards?
- Do you choose your clothing with a motive of drawing attention to yourself?
- Do you know and practice good manners wherever you are?
- Do you tend to want your own way and argue when you do not get it?
- Do you get irritated or exasperated with the character deficiencies of others?
- Do you harbor grudges against those who have hurt you?
- Do you dwell on secret desires to fulfill the lust of the flesh?
- Do you meditate on God's Word day and night and delight to do His will?

How Confirming Testimonies Resulted in a Tenfold Increase in Conversions

After reading the book, The Sevenfold Power of First-Century Churches and Homes, *I decided to incorporate testimonies in our services. For the last few years, we have averaged 13 conversions and baptisms per month. In the last 30 days, we have had 128!*

We have a congregation of about 700, and I suspected that some of the members were not really saved and that others were not properly baptized. Even Charles Spurgeon said that he suspected that fully 50 percent of his congregation was not really saved. I nevertheless am amazed at those who have professed salvation, coming forward weeping, asking to be led in prayer to be saved. Others called at midnight or after hours, with broken hearts, seeking out the pastors in their offices and in their homes to be saved. One man who had come to church for two years said to me, "Pastor, I didn't even hear your message. After that testimony, all I knew was that I needed to be saved."

I attribute our revival to the power of testimonies. I have seen that to forbid opportunities for testimonies is to limit God in being glorified before His congregation. In one service, the testimonies were so powerful that I felt led to give an invitation. Many came forward. It may be that our revival will continue as long as we use the power of testimonies.

Pastor William Yant
from Washington

The physical plant of the church in Pasco, Washington, which is having a dynamic outreach throughout the entire community because of the powerful work of the Holy Spirit within the church.

How a Father Led His Family in First-Century-Type Worship

Implementing this New Testament strategy to experience God's limitless power in our church may take some time, and I am willing to wait to see God do it in His perfect way rather than try to orchestrate some change on my own and watch it flop. On the other hand, I am experiencing a wonderful sense of satisfaction in my own home applying the things I've learned about worship from The Sevenfold Power of First-Century Churches and Homes.

Our family worship has become the highlight of our week and has added a wonderful, exciting dimension to the spiritual oneness and togetherness we have desired for our family. We have been in the ATI program for ten years and taught our children out of the Character Sketches *and Institute material before we enrolled. Our family sings together at Bible conferences and ministers together in hospitals and retirement homes. We have experienced God's power many times in our Wisdom Searches, family devotions, and church worship services.*

However, nothing we have experienced previously compares to the way God has demonstrated His power in our family worship since we began following the first-century Church pattern of worship. Our worship time has become a tangible way for us to see the spiritual growth in each individual family member. God has truly begun to change our hardened hearts. Our hearts had become hardened by the deceitfulness of sin, and God has melted them in our time of family worship. By His grace we are seeking to return to our first love—the Lord Jesus.

Family worship begins each Saturday evening at 7:00 P.M. It is a priority, and everything that takes place on Saturday is considered with family worship in mind. The boys arrange the chairs in the living room, and everyone wears what we are going to wear to church the next morning. We assemble in our kitchen area, and my oldest daughter begins playing a prelude on the piano. I lead the way, and we walk quietly into our makeshift sanctuary, youngest to oldest. I then lead in prayer for our time of worship.

Everyone is seated, and I proceed by quoting a passage of Scripture that the Lord has led me to use for the evening. My goal is to let the Word speak for itself without adding any of my thoughts to it. Following this time in God's Word, I then ask if the Holy Spirit has spoken to anyone concerning the Scripture that was shared.

The insights and personal applications my family is sharing during this special time are the richest times of fellowship in the Word we have ever experienced. There has been open confession of sin, wrong attitudes, and disobedience. As the Spirit leads, I call on a member of the family to pray for the one who has just shared a struggle with sin.

This has become a time of weekly spiritual cleansing for our family as we seek clear consciences with one another and demonstrate full forgiveness toward one another. After this time in the Word we enjoy singing a related hymn, which is enhanced by the flow of joyful tears.

The singing is followed by a teaching time. The character quality we are studying in the Wisdom Booklet has four aspects of its definition in Character Sketches. I briefly cover the lesson from nature and the lesson from Scripture for one of these definitions each week. We then have prayer requests and a time of prayer for our family, our church family, and community leaders.

The benefits of family worship carried out following the pattern of the first-century Church are more numerous than we have discovered. I will list a few of the ones that have been obvious to us:

- *Awareness of the Holy Spirit's working in family members' lives*
- *Opportunity to learn to respond openly without intimidation of strangers*
- *Promotes having a clear conscience and full forgiveness with family members*
- *Experience the joy of sensing the Lord's powerful presence*
- *The blessing of worshiping, singing, and praying in one accord*
- *Prepares you for Sunday morning worship spiritually (worship is more meaningful)*
- *Prepares you for Sunday morning worship practically (clothes are all ready to lay out for dressing the next morning after they get ready for bed; early bedtime)*
- *Opportunity to teach younger children how to behave in church*
- *Strengthens the role of the father as he leads his family to worship*

Richard Gilley
from North Carolina

RESPONSES FROM FAMILY MEMBERS

- *It has been amazing to me to see how the Lord has worked in our family through family worship. When my husband first suggested this idea, it seemed as if it would be another ordinary activity in our already busy schedule. Little did I know how the Lord would use it to open up our hearts to one another and to Him. It has become the highlight of our week! The Spirit has moved in a mighty way as we prayed with and for one another. It has given us the closeness and family harmony that we have always desired.*

Nancy Gilley

- *Family worship has given me an opportunity to share with my family things that the Lord is doing in my life! I have often felt that my friends to whom I write and e-mail knew more about the way my Master is working to conform me to His image than did my parents and siblings. I did not want it to be that way. I longed to share these things with them, but there was never a time when we came together with the purpose of worshiping our great Savior as a family, and giving testimony to His working in our lives. Family worship has given me the freedom to share with my family, and see how the Lord is working in their lives as well!*

  Rebekah, age 15

- *Family worship has drawn our family closer than ever before! It is a wonderful opportunity for us to confess our wrongs and ask forgiveness from other family members. After we share, it means a lot to have a brother or sister pray for you. Daddy always shares an inspiring message from Scripture with us that really encourages me to live closer to the Lord. Then he gives us an opportunity to share testimonies. This time is always very special because it lets us know each other's strengths and weaknesses and gives us a new love for each other.*

  David, age 14

- *I feel as though family worship has drawn me closer to the Lord and to each one in my family. Praying for each other and our specific needs is my favorite part. I remember one of our first family worship services I mentioned my desire to have a closer relationship with Rebekah, my older sister. My dad asked David to pray for me, and the Lord used that prayer to encourage me in this area of my life. I can't wait for family worship time each week!*

  Leah, age 12

- *I enjoy family worship because it gives me a chance to share how God has used His Word in my life. It encourages me to share weak areas in my life that I need to work on. I also enjoyed a few weeks ago when my dad shared about delighting in the Lord from Psalm 37:4. I discovered the truth of that verse since I've learned to delight in Him. He has given me the desires of my heart. I really love family worship.*

Jonathan, age 9

Just as Character Cities must be made up of Character Families, so first-century churches must be composed of families who all follow these principles in their homes